Between Wind and Water

Between Wind and Water

A Devotional For Njord

Edited by Brandon E. Hardy

Hubbardston, Massachusetts

Asphodel Press
12 Simond Hill Road
Hubbardston, MA 01452

Between Wind And Water: A Devotional For Njord
© 2018 Brandon E. Hardy
ISBN 978-1-938197-20-8

Cover Art © 2012 Alexander Baxevanis and © 2011 Motorcat.

All rights reserved. Unless otherwise specified,
no part of this book may be reproduced in any form
or by any means without the permission of the author.

Distributed in cooperation with
Lulu Enterprises, Inc.
860 Aviation Parkway, Suite 300
Morrisville, NC 27560

All proceeds from the sale of this book go to The Gloucester Fishermen's Wives Association. Information about this organization can be found online at gfwa.org. If you have any questions, you can contact the editor at littlemonkfish@gmail.com.

Hail to the Ship-Herd!

Contents

The Cut Of His Jib: Getting to Know Njord

Fathom It Out 1
Goodfather Njord 4
A Letter to Njörðr, Signed Sigyn 6
Njord's Honor 8
Fairy Godfather Njord 13
Meeting Njord 15
Njord, God of Wind, Sea and ... Fire? 18
My Njord Encounter 19
Njord, God of Sailing and Seaports 21
How Njord Came To Asgard 23
Visiting Noatun 30
Learning from Goodfather Njord 33
Njord Sails to Norse Lands 37
Building Bridges 45
Njord the Cold-Hearted Business Man 49

All Hands On Deck: Devotional and Ritual Practices

Ship Herd 55
Charms for Njord 56
A Prayer for the Fishers of Lakes 58
Devotional Ritual for Njord 59
Offerings to Njord 61
Prayer to Njord for Direction 64
Njord's Recipe: Salmon Baked in a Salt Dome 65
Rite of Admiration to Njord 67
Navigating by the Stars 70
Prayer to Njord 71
Invocation to Njord 72
A Prayer for a Strong Ship 75
Hymn to Njord 76
The Vegvisir 77
A Prayer to Njord 79
Njord Ritual: Blessing a Father-To-Be 80

Njord's Frith Prayer 81
Prayer to Njord for Cooperation 82
Fish Wife's Salmon Chowder 83
Blue-Eyed Sailor 85
German Fish Hotpot 86
Ocean Father 87
Boat Blessing Charm 88
The Drowned Dead of the Great Lakes 89
For the Ship-King 90

Note from the Editor

Njord, King of Vanaheim, Protector of Fellow Sailors, Skillful Peacemaker and Warrior, Good Father, Exemplar of Amicable Divorce, Bringer of Wealth, and He Who is Graced with Some Really Nice Feet. A bountiful fisherman renowned for His dedication to His people and His family, it is easy to imagine that He held a place of great reverence in the coastal lands where the worship of the Norse pantheon once flourished.

Yet despite all of this, the majority of the emails that came with the submissions to this devotional spoke to a common theme: while Njord was a beloved and powerful deity, He was still so often passed over in the practice of spiritual and religious communities who worship other Norse deities. Amusingly enough, reading this again and again brought me great hope rather than despair. Seeing so many others motivated by the same sentiment means that this change in the winds is less likely to be fleeting.

After gathering the submissions, it seemed to be a good idea to roughly divide them into two parts. The first section explores Who Njord is to those who honor Him, while the second is a collection of how that honoring can be done. And wonderfully enough, these offered devotions are as varied as the God they are venerating. There are rituals calling upon Him for groups and solo practitioners. There are direct references to well-established lore. There's lore retold with a new voice. There's lore that's actively being recovered. There's poetry and music praising Him. There's recipes. There's tales of a beloved God of old and tales of a God praised today. Even if not all people connect with everything presented in this book (or even downright disagree), it is all a gift to Him, and letting this wide array coexist is in itself an act of devotion to a God who can't be talked about without mention to His role as a negotiator of peace.

So in that spirit of frith-making, I welcome you to this collection of writings for Njord, the Great Ship-King. May this be a place for you to strengthen, or even find, your connection to Him and may you be graced with the warmth of His smile. Hail Njord!

BRANDON E. HARDY
MAY 2017

The Cut Of His Jib: Getting to Know Njord

Fathom It Out
Seawalker

What use is a Lord of Ships, you say,
When Odin's winds are ridden, Thor's storm
Harnessed to your will and wire?
Aye, the ocean still laps the shore, but hardly
Do you think of it, and rivers are to carry
Garbage away, boats are few and far between
And fair forgotten. What need for me, you ask?

Yet the salt tang of the ancestors floats
In the cadence of your languages; so long as
Negotiations are aboveboard, money is made
Hand over fist for the slush fund, which will
Bail you out and tide you over, you keep a log
And know the ropes, you fish for evidence
But are left high and dry; you give a wide berth
To all that takes you aback; so long as
You would be the captain of your own ship,
I have a hook with which to reel you in.
Hook, line and sinker; you cannot strip me
From your sentences. We are in closer quarters
Than you think, and this is by and large
A good thing, as I am the Goodfather,
The peacemaker, for there can be no fair trade
Without peace from shore to shore.

Like all sailors who leave their families at home,
The thoughts of them when the voyage is long
Keep me afloat, and this I can teach to you.
A family can be your anchor when you are all at sea,
But first you must invest, and gather them
If you have few or none, and be worthy.
Commitment is what makes you worthy,

Lads and lasses, even in the face of storms.
For storms pass, and if you wait long enough
The winds will change. Or you will ride them
To another port, and when you return again
Things may be very different, you will see.

So, my sailors, pray for a change of wind,
While you seek family in every new port,
Valuing them all. My wives give me land-legs,
My children, sired and gathered adrift,
Buoy up my heart like the jewels they are.
Even with oceans between us, our love does not fail,
And I teach the lesson of keeping passion
When distance comes between.

I am the light that beckons from the lee shore,
The bridge over troubled waters, the hand
Extended o'er the bargaining cloth, or from
The bow to rescue when you drown.
I am the eyes that search the stars from starboard,
Predicting what will come, for the best course
Should be laid in with full knowledge
Of when to batten hatches, when to catch
The wind of chance. I am the careful one
Who works rather from serenity than panic,
Who rides the fluctuating ocean of feeling
With equanimity and balance, shifting sail
As needed. I do not tame the sea,
Nor ever hope to do so, but I know its ways
And give it offering to stay afloat.

For change is always in the offing,
And you need me when the tides of life
Come hard and fast, to narrowly navigate
Each gale with hope. Let me ever be

The gleaming compass, set with weathered
But still skilled hands, within the hollow
Of your hoary storm-tossed soul.

Goodfather Njord
Galina Krasskova

Njord is perhaps best known in the lore as the father of Frey and Freya and as the husband of Skadhi. It is known that He was Lord of the Vanir and that in order to end the terrible war between the Aesir and Vanir, he agreed to come to Asgard as a hostage. It is through this action, more than any other, that some devotees have come to honor Him as a God of diplomacy and right action. Surely He is a canny diplomat, ruling as He does with relative freedom from the enclave of the Vanir's one-time enemy. He again played the peacemaker when He married Skadhi, after She came seeking vengeance of the Aesir for the death of Her father.

Of course, He is far, far more than that. Njord is God of the shipyard and His hall is called Noatun, which means "ship-yard". From His hands blessings flow: blessing of wealth drawn from the sea. He most especially governs those places where civilization meets the sea and prospers from it. His sacred places are beaches and boats, tidal pools and piers. Because He governs what is given by the sea, I have known many Heathens who have hailed Him as a God of fair commerce and trade. Certainly in my own interactions with Him, I have experienced Njord as a well-tempered God of remarkable equanimity. However, more than any other aspect of His nature, it's Njord the Father that I most often experience, being as I am a devotee of Sigyn.

In fact, that was how I first came to have any kind of relationship at all with Him. Loki told me a story once, which I have passed onto Raven Kaldera for his book *Jotunbok*, about His own first meeting with Sigyn. Through that tale, I was given to know that Sigyn was a foundling, who'd been taken in and raised by Njord. Shortly thereafter, while visiting the Monterey Bay Aquarium, I received an image from Sigyn: Sigyn as a little girl kneeling by a tidal pool, Njord bending over her, hand out-stretched holding a starfish, as he explained the ways of the sea to Her. I saw a little finger reach out to pat the starfish and saw Njord's fatherly smile, and from that moment on I loved Him. Whatever else He may be to others, to me He is Sigyn's Foster-Father, the one who loved and cherished and took care of a Goddess I love beyond breath. Nothing more for me was needed than that.

Of course, I also love Frey and have a respectful relationship with Freya, but even there it was easiest for me to connect to Njord as Their Father. It's often seemed to me that whereas Frey takes after His mother Nerthus with His love of and connection to the land, Freya takes after Her father in Her love of the sea. I often see Her as a young Freya—not a child, but a young woman—walking with Him on the beach. I honor Them both often on the seashore for that reason. I connect best to Freya when I reach out to Her through Njord, just as I first reached Him through Sigyn.

In thinking of Njord, it seems to me that He is a God in whom might and gentleness are equally coupled. I maintain a small shrine to Him (as I also do to Freya, Frey and Gerda) and make offerings to Him regularly whenever I visit the ocean, which is usually every six weeks or so. I make a conscious effort to reach out to Him regularly, to maintain the connection of love and affection that Sigyn so deftly seems to have wrought. Perhaps even more than a God of diplomacy and negotiation, He may be a God of filial and family love, for it seems that in loving and honoring one of His children, I have been led into devotions to all. I bring Him regular gifts of ale, shells and things that I find on the beach, of ocean water and salt, of a compass, music (especially "Fully Rigged" by Aly Bain and Ale Möller), old coins, images of ships and of the sea. At least once a year I take His image—carved out of wood that was once the mast of a ship—to the shore to anoint it with ocean water. Through it all, Njord has become an essential and integral part of my devotional life and above all else, I am grateful.

A Letter to Njörðr, Signed Sigyn
Tahni J. Nikitins

For you, who found me out in the forest all soot-dark, my blood made wild by the shadows at night and the sounds of the beasts in the wood, my voice having forgotten the language of words in favor of the language of screams and hisses.

To you, who found me clothes all ragged and heart all war-weary where the ash still drifted like snow through the bent tree bows like fingers against the graying sky; who found me all small and boney and lifted me out of the hollow of the tree I'd made home and took me back to your riches.

You, mine foster father who called me a girl of victory, whose family was lost to the Great War and who walked away from the slaughter, basically whole if not necessarily well. Alive and surviving I was and under your wing you did take me, you King among the Vanir, who called me daughter with the same voice with which you call Freyja daughter and Freyr son. I, little bones and of hair dark and wild and skin colored like soot, welcomed into the home of the golden ones where it was you, with your hands gentle as safe harbor which helped to pluck the sticks and corpses of insects out of my hair, wash the war off my flesh, and tuck me quiet into a bed made of down.

Giving god that you are, oh foster father mine, you god of wealth bestowed who has bestowed upon me hearth-fire and bread of wheat woven of gold the same as your children's hair—you king among the Vanir who has given me shoes and clothes and roof and wall. Bestowed you upon me such wealth of hearth and home oh you, safe harbor beloved.

Bestow us wealth once more, you peace maker, you forger of unions who places yourself upon the altar of sacrifice (no wonder your son goes so brave to the cutting of the wheat). Go you now with your head held high and your hair all combed, your beard all trimmed, your shoulders humble in their finery and your sea-salt-treated feet carrying you on to Asgard— your altar the altar of peace, your sacrifice an offering of bondage, you father of Freyja and Freyr who follow on your heels. And I the orphan of no known family (lost they to the fire and the blood) follow along, too, in the wake of my beloved foster father and his children who helped me remember the language of words.

Go we now, hostages to peace, riding on down to Asgard and you highest among us, you god of the wain.

For you, who guides the ships into harbor like the lighthouse warding them off of the rocks—it was you I found on the shores off of Asgard, a hostage who is also a king bestowed his own gift: the seashore, a castle built by Jötnar who once called those waves home. Oh, how the landscape of home is ever changing but you, safe harbor, hold my hand and in the quiet of peace you show me the waves. The waves whose only constant is change—the world is never quiet. Even stone dies, crumbled away under the ocean's beat and washed out to sea. But isn't it comforting, knowing we are not the only ones who fall away as dust? Knowing our dust is eternal, recollected from the ocean's bottom into the earth and reborn—

And isn't it comforting, to know none can control the chaos? But the beach here is sandy, where once it was boulders and stony cliff faces like the bones of giants, and the sand is soft. I follow your footprints along the shore and watch the waves crack like whips against the stones jutting out of the water out there, the hungry teeth of the Wave-Maidens ready to snap and jaw when the ships come passing by. Oh, how they love to eat.

But here is safe harbor.

You, who will become Skadi's groom (it is lonely here, this unfamiliar place) you maker of peace and giver of wealth—give me more. Another hearth, another home—I am out of place, here, with my little bones and black-ish hair and blood that remembers the wild. And you ... you will give me a husband who breathes fire into my bone-cold cheeks and brings a blushing laugh to my lips which once only knew the language of screams and hisses.

This is for you, my foster father who bestowed on me such wealth as this—a hearth, a home, a family, an eye for the crashing waves of the sea. These are my thanks given only to you, you king among the Vanir who guides the ships safely home—my dearest beloved Njörðr, who has given me all of this.

Even with all that is to come, at least you've given me the chance to know this. At least I've known this.

Njord's Honor
Bernulf Oswin

The presentation of Njord in the Eddas is not necessarily the most inspiring or honorable. In *Gylfaginning*, we are told that "...the Vanir delivered him as hostage to the gods" as an atonement for the war between Æsir and Vanir. *Gylfaginning* goes on to tell us that Njord was once married to Skadi, but neither could abide moving to the other's home, since Njord lived by the sea and Skadi lived in the cold mountains. They came to the arrangement of spending each nine days and nights in the other's home before switching, but we are told that Njord could not tolerate even nine days in the mountains, preferring the song of swans to the howling of wolves. For her part, Skadi couldn't tolerate the "wailing" of sea gulls; it disturbed her sleep, and she much preferred hunting in the mountains. This led to the end of the marriage.[1]

In *Skáldskaparmal*, we are told how it came to be that Njord and Skadi were married. After the gods killed Skadi's father, the giant called Thjazi, Skadi donned armor and weapons and resolved to have her revenge in Asgard. The gods were loathe to do battle with Skadi, so they asked for her terms for peace. Her first term was that she be allowed to choose from among the Æsir a husband, and her second term was that she be made to laugh. The gods agreed to this, and made the condition that Skadi could only choose her husband by seeing his feet. When the gods lined up, Skadi chose the prettiest feet she could find, thinking they belonged to Baldr ... but it turned out that she chose Njord.[2]

These descriptions of Njord seem humiliating; he is sent by the Vanir as a hostage, then chosen by a giantess by the beauty of his feet. The entire story of how Njord and Skadi came to be married is seen as a story that inverts traditional gender roles, which seems only the more

---

[1] *Gylfaginning*, XXIII
[2] *Skáldskaparmal* p. 91-92

humiliating for Njord.³ To make matters worse, in *Lokasenna*, Njord is accused by Loki of incest—having a son by his sister—and is also accused of being defiled by the daughters of the sea-giant, Hymir.⁴

So, with all of these things taken together, it would seem almost as though Njord's standing among the mighty Æsir should be pretty low—but in fact it isn't. In *Gylfaginning*, Njord is named third among the Æsir, after Thor and Baldr—a pretty lofty status, actually. Njord is also called upon for voyages and hunting—two very important activities among our Heathen forebears. Finally, Njord is said to be so rich that he can afford to give great amounts of land and gear to those who call upon him for it. Keep in mind with this that the honor of kings and chieftains among the Norse was often dependent on their wealth and generosity. So we have the beginnings of a very interesting contradiction within the Eddas. A god who is at once considered weak, passive, and in some ways feminine—yet is counted third among the gods, is depended upon for important things, and has an unimaginable amount of wealth. To solve this contradiction, I will rely on other sources that are fairly uniform in their regard for Njord.

First, I would point out that it isn't just among the Æsir that Njord holds such high status. In looking at place names in the Scandinavian region, we see that place names in Norway for Njord outnumbered those for Odin nearly two-to-one.⁵ We are also told that, along with either Odin or Thor, Njord and his son, Freyr, were invoked when taking public oaths—a practice which continues in current times among Heathens.

Viktor Rydberg identifies Njord with Fridleif (from Saxo Grammaticus), and credits him with being not just the chief of the Vanir, but also the one responsible for defeating the original defenses of Asgard.⁶ There are a couple of descriptions of Njord from Rydberg that I will quote here:

---

³ Lindow, John (2001), *Norse Mythology* p. 242, Santa Barbara, Oxford University Press
⁴ *Lokasenna* p.163
⁵ Cherry, Nicole (2001), *Norse Mythology* (Njord)
⁶ Rydberg, Viktor (1889), *Teutonic Mythology* chapter 36

Njörðr klauf Herjans hurðir – "Njord broke Odin's doors open"
Gauts megin-hurðar galli – "the destroyer of Odin's great gate"
(This second reference is a kenning for the battle-axe, and thus connects Njord to the battle-axe.)

I would also point out at this point that the name Fridleif translates into "lover of peace", and Njord's son Freyr is often identified with the king Frodhi, also known for peace and plenty. So what we are given by Rydberg's interpretation is that we have a god, a chief among the Vanir, who is by nature a lover of peace (as indicated by the name) and prosperity. This much is also supported by the Eddas. However, when angered and driven to war, he is powerful and clever enough to threaten Asgard itself, and cause the Æsir to sue for peace.

The other thing I will point out at this time is the accusation of incest by Loki in *Lokasenna*, where Njord is accused of begetting a son from his own sister (Njord is only one of several gods Loki insults in this story). We are told in the Eddas that incest was something permitted among the Vanir, but rejected by the Æsir ... but we are not given the exact nature of the incest. By Norse reckoning, a man's sister-in-law would also be seen as and referred to as "sister", and for a man to have romantic relations with her would be construed as incest. The same could also apply to the sister of a blood-brother. So the incest referred to here may not be quite as drastic as it appears at first glance. The other thing to consider here is that the Vanir are nature deities. Njord is the fertile coastal areas, where the land meets the sea. He does not dwell in the sea, as does Ægir, but near it in his ship yard. A related goddess, Nerthus, is often identified as being the unnamed sister of Njord (sometimes also as Njord, himself), and Nerthus is regarded also as a sea or coastal deity, so it is possible that the incestuous relationship cited is an Æsir-dominated reaction to how the cult of Vanir regarded the relationship between land and sea. There are scholars who believe that the entire war between the gods is a takeover myth, describing the incorporation of the cult of the Vanir into the more dominant cult of the Æsir. So the relationship between sea and land argument is viable in this situation, and would also explain the need for Njord to be humbled in the Eddas, so that he does not draw glory or attention away from Odin or the other Æsir.

Considering the importance of Njord among our Heathen forebears—by way of oathing, areas of dependency, wealth-giving and place names—we have a god who can claim great honor. That he is credited with basically winning the war against the Æsir should also indicate that this is not a god of weak-willed nature. That he is honored hostage among the Æsir is not a matter of debate; but to contrast the description in *Gylfaginning* with the descriptions given by Rydberg and Saxo, I would say that a chief among the Vanir would give himself as hostage, not be handed over. This would be a great sacrifice for Njord to make, and it must have been done to ensure peace among the gods at a time when he could have simply defeated the Æsir (that the Æsir were defeated by the Vanir is also attested to in the Eddas).[7] Looking at all of this, it's easier to understand why such effort is undertaken to humiliate Njord in the Eddas, and why Njord's honor is greater and deeper than how it may be reflected on the surface to some.

(This article was originally published on 16 August, 2006, in my blog, Noatún; then republished on 30 December 2006, in A Heathen Blog: Expanding Inward, *where it can still be found in its original form. This version has been altered from its original in order to change the format from blog form to something more suitable for printing. Permission to reprint has been granted to Asphodel Press by Bernulf Oswin/Stormwise Raven in 2016 for charity purposes.)*

---

[7] *Voluspo*, st. 23 (p. 11)

Lacking a decisive symbol for Njord, Bernulf Oswin, author of the piece proceeding this, created an axe head / ship hybrid symbol to fill that need. The image above builds off of the initial design. Going from top to bottom, the first Rune is a mirror-imaged Fehu, representing wealth and His children Freya and Frey. The knot below it is built off of Inguz, which is both the Rune of sacrifice and His son Frey. There are stones in the place of stylized shields to involve Njord's sacred number of five. The Runes on the side of the ship (and their keywords) are Gifu (gift), Mannaz (community), Laguz (water), and Uruz (strength). Through their meanings they express the sentence: Give to the people in troubled water an anchor. - Brandon E. Hardy

Fairy Godfather Njord
Linda Demissy

Received at a spirit supper to Njord on July 10, 2016

My friends, when you hear of Thor's adventures, your mind's eye shows the giants he faced; his companion Loki, getting him in and out of trouble. But the one you never see is Njord. Yet how does Thor get to Jotunheim? His chariot cannot cross the rainbow bridge without setting it aflame. Unless they use the Hel-road, they must go by boat. Whose boat? Njord's, of course.

"Load the chariot aboard," Thor says, "and let us sail to Jotunheim, for there is adventuring to be done!" Or somewhere else, but usually Jotunheim.

"As you wish," says Njord with a smile, making sure they have enough provisions, for he has grown to love Thor like a son, and it's a good excuse to get out of Asgard for a while. And when they arrive, Njord always says: "This time, I'd like to go with you, and help on your adventure."

"No, my friend," answers Thor with a pat on the back, "you stay here with the boat, old man, and make sure it is safe for our return. We would not want you to be in danger in these lands. And now, we are off to adventure!"

"As you wish," answers Njord with a sad smile.

He was treated as the "uncool" parental figure and left behind, so he's not in the stories. Yet he was there. When Loki and Thor were tired and hungry, there would be an abandoned house with a lit fire waiting for them. As if by magic. And some fishes drying outside on a rack.

"How lucky we are," Thor would exclaim each time.

"I know!" Loki answered as he set to cooking the meal.

Or when they were outnumbered, there would be a loud noise distracting some of the giants away. Very coincidentally.

And when Thor needed to make a guest gift, somehow there was always something appropriate in his pouches that he didn't remember putting there.

And somehow, the giants they met were usually well disposed toward the two visitors, with a feast made ready, as if they were expected—as if some wanderer had mentioned their coming. What good fortune they had!

When they came back and told their tale, Thor said how fortunate Njord was to have been spared the hardships of the journey, staying comfortable on his boat. And Loki, well, he winked at Njord. He knew what was up. Because on each night of the journey while Thor slept soundly, Njord crept up to the fire to warm himself. There, he and Loki would whisper of what was needed for the day ahead, of the best places and those to avoid from what Njord had scouted out.

"Don't tell him I was here," Njord would say every time before he left.

"I know, Good Father," Loki always answered, amused by the trickery that made him look like Thor's lucky charm. "It would ruin Thor's fun to know someone's looking out for him."

So now, when you hear of Thor's adventure, you'll know of the hidden figure, the one that is never mentioned. And because he behaved like the Hidden Folk, the Fairy Folk, we say that Njord is Thor's Fairy Godfather.

Meeting Njord
Joshua DeVault

January mornings are always a bit cold and foreboding when looking outside. For three nights, I went to sleep with prayers to Niorun and Odin with the intent to meet Njord. What beautiful dreams transpired! The first one introduced me to the Puffin. In the second one I was working with ocean animals at an aquarium, and the third one had to do with a seashell.

Sipping on my hot coffee while looking at the crows peck at the birdfeeder relaxed me into my cozy blanket and hoodie. I finally got the message: it was time to meet Him. I have been trying to meet with Njord ever since his energy connected to mine. It's really hard to put this into words—how do you know a God wants to work with you? Well, you just do. While I could bully myself with the "Why didn't I come see him sooner?" question—like a year ago when that call first came into my life—I didn't. He never brought it up either.

I turned on some relaxing background music, sank into my warm blanket, put my hood just over my eyes, and started to drift. It's almost like sleep, except that your mind is awake and your body is asleep. I was aware of my still body, I would intend to move my hand, but when it didn't move I knew it was time for the image work.

First, the image of a lighthouse came to mind. I could hear the seagulls singing their tunes, and the salty (and occasionally fishy) smell of the ocean came to me. Soon after this I found a little rowboat which I got into and laid down and stared up at the clouds, taking in all the smells and sounds around me.

Even though my hour was spent talking with Njord, I never actually saw him. I just heard his voice amidst the seagulls, and felt the waves rocking the boat gently while I looked up at the lighthouse and sky. He answered questions that have been on my mind for some time. Within my spiritual path, he clarified that I am on the path of the frith-maker, the peacemaker, and he wanted to help me.

We discussed briefly about how his whole family can teach about different aspects of Love. I have worked passionately with Frey in the past, and it was implied that he had a helping hand in getting me into connection with his Father. Maybe it was Frey's idea for us to meet in the first place? After this point of connection on the familiar, we delved into the unfamiliar. Njord wanted to make it very clear that I am on a path of the frith-maker, and not on a "path of secrets". In pushing for more information on this, it was discussed that his wife teaches the way of secrets, but his way is not that path. All that I learn should, and needs to be, shared and taught to help others grow and build up their communities. No secrets, no mysteries, just open and frank talks.

I got the impression that the wife he was discussing was not Skadi. We were talking about the love nature of his Vana family. Is this the Nerthus I hear about as Vanaheim's Earth Mother? Anyway, Njord had a sense of humor because the way he talked about his "wife of secrets" was like any other man might talk about his wife. This Vana wife seems to be scary, as it was very clear that her way was not my path and I shouldn't at this point even give thought to the prospect of meeting her.

Our conversation continued to talk about the concept of love in Community. This was about not physical or emotional love, or attachment of the kind western culture talks about. It is hard to put it in words, but seemed like a fraternal bond. It speaks of every person in the community having an integral skill and necessity for being there. Every person in the community is sacred, and with their integral part, the community is made whole. If one person leaves or dies, it is beyond just missing one person, it is the lack of their presence and very essence.

This is the sense of his "Love" aspect that I recognized - the power of bonds and the power of community. Maybe "extreme friendship" is a better way to describe this path? Later, he might help me to help others understand their place in the community, but there is a lot to do before that. Our conversation continued to a specific magical teaching he offers— the power of the handshake. While it may seem cheesy to call it magical, the way he described it was fascinating. A handshake is the first point of contact from person to person. It starts friendship, it shows trust, it is a cultural way to enhance business transactions, and even is involved in weddings (handfastings). So while giving a handshake, you should transfer a bit of your energy to another person. With practice, the intention should be unconditional love for the stranger. This is a very powerful form of frith. While you are shaking hands, your view of the person should be about how their skills or services can help the community. Your handshake energy exchange must transmit the unconditional love of your community and introduce its values and integrity to the other person. You should focus on extreme positive intent to see a good end result, whether a trade agreement or friendship. It is a form of hospitality—welcoming the stranger with goodwill.

I got excited at all this handshake talk, and asked him how soon I could start learning this? Njord laughed a little, and told me that it wouldn't be any time soon. What he has to offer is not an easy path. He brought up the fact that he has major concerns about my energy body, and he felt that that should be my first concern. Working with my energy and learning to cleanse negativity should be a priority. I would also need to have complete mastery in understanding Wyrd—how it interacts with the self, and all the ancestral blessings and burdens it may imply. Next would be understanding how this Wyrd works within a small group, and eventually a community. Lastly the frith-maker should understand the interaction of wyrd with such things as the land, hospitality, and the relationship of agreements with people and spirits. Njord made it clear that there is a lot more to all this, and it was well beyond my ability to comprehend at this point.

I woke up and finished my cold coffee. It was an hour later—the most time I have ever spent with a non-patron deity or spirit. The next day I saw a seagull flying in a parking lot, and while not too many people would call the bird majestic, it was a graceful creature. The song of the seagull made me feel connected to the ocean again, and I was reminded not to be overwhelmed by everything in front of me, but rather take it with one wave at a time. I thought of words from the poet Kahlil Gibran: "Love one another, but make not a bond of love. Let it rather be a moving sea between the shores of your souls."

Njord, God of Wind, Sea and ... Fire?
Heather Awen

> *The third Ás is the one called Niord. He lives in heaven in a place called Noatun. He rules over the motion of wind and moderates sea and fire. It is to him one must pray for voyages and fishing. He is so rich and wealthy that he can grant wealth of lands or possessions to those that pray to him for this.*
>
> -*Edda,* Snorri Sturluson (Antony Faulkes translation)

I never see the fire aspect included in books' descriptions of Njord. I've known that his magic is wind magic, like women tying knots and selling them to sailors. First knot as a breeze instead; untie and it's released. Second knot a strong headwind. Third, which no one probably untied very often, a raging gale.

However, he moderates fire?

Then I read a very well-researched historical fiction book called *The Hall of Tyr* by Octavia Randolph. In a trading town in Gotland the tar maker's building erupts into flames, taking more buildings with it as the fire spread. Everyone, no matter who, became part a chain of humans handing bucket, cauldron, pot, anything of sea water from shore to fire. It was the ocean water they had to use to put out the fire. Empty containers went back to the people at the shore and were refilled. This went on for hours.

Now I get it. Njord was so much more important than Heathens or even Vanatru give him credit for. Part of it is living away from the shore. But he's still the chieftain of the Vanir and Priest of the Aesir. Global warming has caused wind patterns to change, which means hurricanes and wild fires. If you're involved with any type of Engaged Paganism about Global Warming, Njord is your allied deity.

My Njord Encounter
Ember Cooke

I was on my way to Wyrmholm for Stitch-N-Bitch, and swung through Hayward on the way to wait for David to catch up with me. Of course, being me, I waited in Starbucks. I'd brought a book in, but I'll take a conversation over a book most of the time, so I was quite content for the fellow occupying one of the two comfortable chairs to chat with me. I was, however, startled that he started it—I'm used to being the one to strike up the conversation.

He was an older fellow, maybe in his seventies. Narrow frame, white hair, lovely blue eyes, and all smiles and charm. He had been born in Norway, but was raised in the US. His mother wanted him to be a minister, but he was called to join the Navy, and there spent most of his career. Even now, he's an officer in the reserve, because he enjoys the work, but is too old for full-time. His main job now is as a night banker, handling the accounts between transaction phases. He's also a teacher of math because he enjoys instructing and motivating young people. His wife is departed, though he looks forward to being with her again when he passes on. In the meantime he's keeping company with a wonderful woman who understands things.

Most of the conversation simply amused me, because he was quite charming and personable, and very cheerful. He asked me questions about how things were for me, and we passed the time. But what struck me very strongly, emotionally, and made me realize that I'd just been chatting with an old blue-eyed sailor born in Norway was when, after David showed up, the old fellow explained how proud he was to hear that I was going to graduate with two AAs this June. For just a moment I felt as though he'd known me for years, as if I were some relative of his, not a total stranger he started talking to less than an hour ago. And I recognised that Goodfather Njord had just sent me a message I hadn't been listening for directly.

When I got to Wyrmholm, I was inspired to make a new necklace for Njord, and I've been wearing it a lot lately. But Njord doesn't seem very talkative. He's been comforting, and supportive, but not usually very chatty.

I've found Him, in the past, to be the kind of fellow who is very slow to temper—partially because He just plain likes people, and partially because He is very patient, but also because He has a fair amount of experience with women who have rather quick tempers, and has learned that the best way to handle other people losing theirs is to keep your own.

He enjoys the look on someone's face when He gives them a treasure they never expected to receive, or something amazing they'd never even heard of before—especially His wives and children. I have a sense that He dotes on Freya—first when She was a young girl, bringing Her lovely things, and then later, more protectively, when She grieved for Od.

And Njord has offered me help for my own father, whose luck as an entrepreneur hasn't been what it could be. He's expressed a willingness to help my father "bring his ships in"—literally: I was instructed that we should get together and made a model long ship, and set it to water, with his hopes in the hold.

Njord, God of Sailing and Seaports
Heather Awen

My relationship with Njord is really colored with my relationship with my family. My grandmother came from fishing families that fished in the Irish Sea, which is one of the most toxic waters around, a point that people should be concerned about. But back then, of course, the big concern was drowning, which did have a lot of impact on my ancestry. That actually comes under a different deity, as drowning is done by Ran, not Njord, but Njord obviously was the provider for my family as the god of fishermen.

Then I lived on a boat from age sixteen to age seventeen. There were a couple of fishermen in the boatyard, one from Ireland and one from Scotland, who would speak in Gaelic and were a lot of fun to hang out with, as well as other fishermen going about their routines, so I sort of became part of that culture.

My dad loves sailing, especially in scary weather, which kind of turned me off to the boats for a while. (His side of the family has all the Vikings.) But I loved living on them; I loved the rocking of the waves and the water. I went on the ferries across the North Sea and across the Irish Sea, and I couldn't even handle those very well, as everyone was smoking hash and drinking, and I have too many bad memories of being twelve and trapped in a cabin with that. A cabin is the last place you want to be when you're chronically ill.

The other side of Njord is commerce, and that was something I didn't really understand, but I've been reading all the new stuff that people are finding out about history, and Ireland is embracing a lot more of its Viking heritage. Maybe that's just because it's a trend, what with TV shows about the Vikings. But I have an ancestor on my dad's side, King Olaf the White, a Norseman who ruled Dublin, and was married to Aud the Deep-Minded in the sagas. I'm also related to the sister of Ivar the Boneless. In Ireland, two cities—including Dublin—were built by the Vikings because when you want to control access to the water, you want big well-defended ports, not just inland cities.

Reading about what Dublin was like during this time period when my ancestors were founding and running it, I realized it was somewhere I'd really want to be. Although I grew up really rural, in the middle of nowhere, and learned a lot of homesteading skills like milking goats and tapping trees and planting things and identifying weeds and all that outdoorsy survival stuff, white people are so boring, and the rural area I was in was all WASPs. So when I was a teenager I went to London and squatted there during the poll tax riot, and it was just like, culture culture culture! Lots of languages, lots of different customs. Today, you can get everything on the Internet and you don't have to go anywhere, but back then you had to travel to find interesting things and people. So I really appreciate Njord on two different levels—as a god of cosmopolitan multicultural trade cities, and as the god that supported my ancestors who lived there.

How Njord Came To Asgard
Linda Demissy

When the war the Aesir waged against the Vanir came to an end, hostages were exchanged. The Vanir chose to invest their most powerful and important gods in this trade, to give the Vans a strong voice in the decisions of Asgard. Thus they hoped this arrangement would bring profit to both realms. Freya was to court Odin, who hungered for her knowledge of seidh magic. Frey would befriend Thor, and Njord would ally with Frigga, who had been a decisive player in bringing about this peace. Their homeland was left in the hands of the wise and mighty Nerthus.

Just as Njord and Frey were not counted among the Aesir gods back then, so too were goddesses missing from the Asynjur court. Syn, the one who guards, was not yet one of them. Thus the role of protecting Frigga and her domain of Fensalir was given to Hlin—the hero who mourns. Only Gna—messenger of the spirits—was also trained in battle, but she was more suited to the role of skirmisher than protector.

Farewells were spoken and many tears were shed when Hoenir and Mimir departed in their ship for Vanaheim. Frigga gave Fulla rulership of her court so she could spend time in private meditation. To Snotra she gave the task of welcoming and preparing a feast in Fensalir. Hlin was ordered to greet the sea god Njord and determine his worth, to uncover whether he was a true ally or a threat to their court.

Each day after that, Frigga took the White Forest Path from Fensalir to the sauna that stood among birches. There she sought visions in the clouds of steam, of the future and how to adapt her plans to peacetime.

It was also time for farewells in Vanaheim. Njord straightened out his blue tunic and sighed as he faced his ship. Broad for cargo, yet also blessed with beautiful carvings and gold gilding, the Drunken Star was perhaps not the best of ships ... but its railing was worn smooth by his loving caresses. He glanced back at familiar hills beyond the harbor, then gazed downriver to the sea. Once he boarded it, the *Drukkin Stjarna* would be his only home. Perhaps Asgard would eventually become one as well, but the Golden Realm of Plenty would never again be his own.

"Father?" Freya said with a hand on his shoulder, her golden sleeve drooping along his arm.

"I am a selfish man," he said, "for I cannot endure this exile without my children. I do not mind sacrificing my freedom for peace, but how can I bear the guilt of bringing you both along with me?"

"Nonsense, Father," she answered. "Our three voices will be loud in the courts of the White Realm, craftily leading them to our way of thinking, and I shall wrench Odin's secret rune spells for myself."

"If you look the other way," said green-clad Frey with a grin, "we can hide as stowaways, and then you will bear no blame for our coming."

Eyes moist, he embraced his children and led them aboard.

Odin was at the front of the welcoming party on the grassy shores of Asgard when they docked, deep blue cloak over a gray robe, a wide brimmed hat hiding his eyes. To his left, red-bearded Thor stood, scratching at what seemed a brand new and still itchy brick-colored tunic. To his right, dressed in the blue of evening sky was Tyr, the ancient Jotun sky god who had betrayed his people to stand with the Aesir. Spear in hand, his eyes were shaded half-shut, watchful of the proceedings. Many more warriors formed a half-circle behind them, clad in chain mail with spears at the ready.

Frigga and her ladies were nowhere to be seen, Njord noticed in dismay. A single woman stood on the wooden pier, with the size and brawn to rival any soldier there. She had a roughly woven sea-blue dress under loose-fitting ring mail, and a staff tipped with iron strapped to her back. It was she who caught the rope he threw, meeting his eyes with a stoney gaze before tying it to the mooring post with a proper sailor's knot. The gods greeted and led away his children to a great feast in their honor, leaving only the sullen and silent Hlin before him, squinting with suspicion. She had been mistress of all maritime matters until then—as the daughter of a sea goddess and an Aesir man—and this newcomer was a challenge to her authority. It gave her all the more reason to dislike him.

"Hail to you, God of Ships," she finally said with only the hint of a bow.

"And hail to you, Daughter of Ran. Where is your Mistress?" he asked in puzzlement. "I have brought many guest-gifts for the Queen and those of your court who helped orchestrate this peace. I look forward to giving her proper honor if you'll but lead me to her and–"

"She is occupied with private matters that take precedence," Hlin interrupted. "You will have to wait here until she is ready."

"I– ah... yes, I shall wait," he agreed.

When it was clear she would say no more, he sighed and went back to his ship. There he prepared presents, praise, and many offers of assistance to ingratiate himself with the Queen of the land, as the proper peacemaker that he was. Hlin remained on the shore to keep watch over him and see what he would do.

The next few days did not go well for Njord.

Frigga remained locked in meditation, so he tried making nice with the one who barred his way—but she would have none of it, and gave Njord a hard time in a thousand small and large ways. Resenting his presence and suspicious of his motives, he watched and wept as his priceless gifts were dismantled for possible traps and curses.

He tried to go around her, slip in to see Frigga so this silliness could be resolved. But each time he did, the goddess of preparedness thwarted him. She planned for every sneaky thing he could do, and with each attempt became more convinced of his treachery. He was skilled in diplomacy and court intrigues, but knew little of stealth and deceit without courtiers to carry them out. She was warrior-trained and had spent many years hiding her half-giantess lineage among mortals, so he was no match for her.

In other words, she trounced him soundly. Repeatedly.

Yet there was one from Frigga's court who offered him welcome during that first week. Snotra—goddess of wisdom, hospitality and elevation—was moved to act, though she could not greet him officially. So she came upon a plan of her own.

Each day at sunset, Hlin returned to the great wall surrounding Asgard proper for her supper, giving Njord the illusion of privacy so he would reveal his motives. And each day, he spied a brown-haired lass with two bowls of steaming stew, looking out to sea. She contrasted with the armed men that paced about, her sky-blue apron belted over a white dress without any embellishing embroidery. He assumed she was a servant, and in his frustration, hoped he might use her as tool to reach Frigga. So it was not the god of peace who approached her that first day, but a man mired in schemes, willing to act dishonorably to achieve his goals.

"Ah, you are not the one," she said sadly as she looked into his eyes. "I have arrived too late, or perhaps too early."

"Are you waiting for someone?" he asked, putting thumbs into his belt to avoid looking threatening.

"Yes," she said with a nod, "I am waiting for a friend."

When she said nothing more, he asked. "Tell me of this friend, that I might recognize them when I see them."

"Well, he is a sailor, an honest man with a kind face, always ready to offer help to those in need. A man of virtue and integrity who sees the best in people and lives with hope in his heart. His ship was to arrive today, but I am sorry to see he is not yet here. I came to share a welcome meal with him, and celebrate his arrival."

Touched by her words, Njord nodded. "Such a man is indeed worthy of welcome and rejoicing. I hope for your sake that he arrives soon."

She smiled again briefly, like the sunlight that flickers upon the face of hasty travelers under a canopy of leaves. "Since he is not here, and I am laden with two meals, would you like to share them with me?"

The rumble of his stomach answered for him, and she laughed as he blushed. "Yes, I believe I'd enjoy that very much. What should I call you?"

"My friends call me Snow," she said as she offered him the bowl which was slightly fuller than the other. "Will you bless the food, kind sir, before we eat?"

His mouth watered, grasping the bowl tightly, but he declined. "I would rather allow you to do so, kind lady, for I am a stranger in this land and would like to learn your ways." At last, he thought, a friendly face among foes.

Again her smile flickered, and she nodded, then spoke:

"Hear me my relations, from the first to the last,
Sacred ones whose sacrifice fed our people.
Since Audhumla was freed has your blood and milk flowed,
So I grieve for your death, grateful words for your gifts.
May your spirits be blessed, in abundance abide,
In the next life knowing your flesh nourished mine."

They ate and they talked, and though deflecting questions about Asgard, she was endlessly interested in stories of his homeland. He learned little from her, yet found solace at her side and was inspired by her counsels. Among these, she mentioned how cats are tamed; not by trying to catch them but by letting them come to you. He thought of Toby, his beloved ship's cat, and how this might work with Hlin.

After that first week he gave up on the direct route, diplomacy, and deceit. The more subtle his peacemaking became, the more she thought him manipulative. So he tried an entirely different approach. He set himself up in a hut by the shore, refusing to speak to anyone or eat anything.

Hlin spied on him for days, expecting a trick. But he had no tricks. He just got thinner and weaker. For twenty-one days she went out of her mind trying to figure out what he was up to. She finally burst into the shack and demanded to know what he was doing. He spoke for the first time in three weeks, being quite emaciated and weakened by then.

"I will eat only when Frigga herself offers to share her food."

Hlin's jaw dropped. But at the same time, she could see he was too weak to be a threat to anyone. She went back to consult with Frigga.

The queen was at the time coming out of the sauna when Hlin arrived, shaken from a terrible vision: that peace would be broken, that war would blaze once more, and that her adopted son Thor would perish.

"Tell me Hlin, for I must know," said Frigga, her eyes haggard and hair matted with sweat, "though I failed to greet him myself as was proper. Has Fulla insulted Njord while he supped in Fensalir? Has Snotra failed to bring him the foods he favors? Or is he feasting with his children in Valhalla under Odin's care? Tell me quickly, for I must speak with him and find what flaw in our welcome will bring us doom."

Blushing in shame and horror, Hlin told her he was still on the shore in a hut, refusing all food until Frigga herself shared her meal, and that she had not allowed him into the realm.

"Why didn't you let him come see me, all this time?"

"I didn't trust him," replied Hlin. "He was constantly scheming."

"He was scheming because you wouldn't let him speak to me. Have a meal prepared and send it after me. I'm going to the shore."

"But ... there is no security! I must stay with you—" But Frigga just gave her a withering glare that allowed no argument. Hlin swallowed and went to assemble a plate of food as fast as she could.

Frigga walked slowly down the road to the shore, thinking of what she'd say. When she opened the door and saw the state he was in, she wept. And when Njord noticed her, he smiled. His voice was coarse and weak when he spoke.

"If I'd known you were coming," he said with a wry grin, "I would have washed. Here I am, grimy before the queen, and the sea's but a skip away." He tried to rise, but couldn't, so she came in and helped him sit. She apologized for his mistreatment, and he countered that she wasn't to blame.

Hlin arrived to the scene of Njord in Frigga's arms, and winced before offering the plate of food. Frigga broke a piece of bread, and offered him some, but his mouth was so parched that he could not get it into his mouth. So she chewed it for him, and gave it like a mother bird to her child—with a kiss. He thanked her, took a sip from her cup, then looked to Hlin who stood there mortified by the situation she had caused.

Frigga gave Hlin a glare. "You will have to answer for the harm you caused, Hlin. Had he died, the war would have started again. I foresaw this. So as punishment, you will..."

Njord coughed then and said: "She is not to blame either. No good will come of inflicting misery for mistakes made in earnest devotion. She was protecting you to the best of her ability." He grinned. "And it has been a long time since I've been so well-treated by a queen. Peace is worth a little of my suffering."

"What do you suggest then, Sea God?" asked Frigga.

"How about this? Whenever your court has need of me, have Hlin bring me some of your meal as a gesture of goodwill and friendship. For when we share food, our bellies are united in wishing for peace and plenty. Could I have some more now, please?"

Frigga smiled. "Very well, but I'll not chew it for you this time."

He gave her sad eyes. She relented, and gave him one more bite that way. Maybe two.

Visiting Noatun
December Fields-Bryant

The dock is surrounded by mist. There is a creaking sound as the wood groans against the tide coming in. The smell of salt and fish is pungent in the air and the light breeze coming off the water has a chill that speaks of distant, snowy mountains and deep, sunless waters. I cross my bare arms against my chest, wishing I had a wrap or a quilt even, and missing my Lady's hearth. Yet I step forward, bare feet feeling the grain of the wood planks and grit of salt and fish scales.

Behind me, Hlin stands sentry. I had asked her and my Lady why I needed a protectress with me—would Njord do me harm? Hlin only gave a half-smile and the smallest shake of her head. She gave me no promises but explained that this was simply how things were done among the diplomats of Fensalir and Noatun. I kept that in mind as I walked down the dock and tried to feel reassured.

My hands feel particularly empty. I have no cake of salt or shell of incense, no bread or ale to offer Him. I have only myself, dressed far too simply for this excursion. I chide myself for not planning ahead. I should know by now that if I go to Frigga to ask about another of the Gods, that rather than give me a simple explanation, she will quickly send me off to ask that God of himself instead. Hasn't this happened often enough that I should know by now?

The wind picks up as I near the end of the dock. I feel salt spray on my face and arms. My long skirt whips about my legs. Tendrils of hair that have escaped my head cover are wet and whip against my face and neck. I can taste it on my lips and in my breathing.

I wonder again why I am here. I have not been called by Njord. Is this a trip of curiosity? Is it sacrilege? No. Seeking knowledge with respect isn't shameful. I think of my own husband and my son, of the days my beloved goes to ocean-fed rivers to catch salmon so that we can be nourished. I think of his Piscean nature and love of water and boats. I think of his astrology chart and his risk of dying due to water. Njord is a god I would do well to honor.

I steel my nerves as I turn to the boat.

The boat was large and flat, not what I expected. I supposed I was thinking he would be working on an ancient Viking ship. This looked like those boats that river rats in city canals live on, scrounging up whatever they can find caught in the dams and ports. Nets and other fishing gear litter the sides. Njord is there, near the back by a rectangular box where I presume he rests and stores his things. He is cutting up the day's catch. The smell of fresh fish is strong.

When he does look up and acknowledge me, giving me permission to come aboard, I am taken aback by his features. His face is rough-hewn and strong as stone. His beard is short but thick and damp with salt water, as are his brows. His hair is long and pulled back with a leather thong. His eyes stop me from moving or speaking. I have to look away, but they still burn cold within me. They are blue-green and speak of ocean storms and depths I cannot fathom. My heart is pounding as I step carefully from dock to boat.

He showed me a fishing fetish—a leather bag that is carefully and continuously treated with oils as the salt water and wind makes the leather crack easily. The strap is braided hemp cord. I open the back; the closure is made from cord and bead. Within is an effigy of Njord carved into stone. Its smooth from water-wear and touch. I turn it in my hand and it is now drift wood with the same carving. Either will do, I understand. This totem is continuously baptized in the salty waters.

Njord explains that he takes offerings of handmade bread. I see fisher wives baking the yeasty, dark brown loaves. Ale and light beer with bitter flavors are favored. Cakes of salt, carefully harvested salt rock and waters, and strings of shells can be arranged lovingly on altars with Njord's image. Hearty meals and songs that match the rhythmic tides are favored on his feast days. He enjoys working by the moon and is well acquainted with Mani.

I thank him, telling him I will bring this back to my husband so that he might stitch these practices into the fabric of his life. I stand to go but stop. Head down, I ask if he wants anything of me. I am no fisher and water frightens me. I have nothing to offer him myself except for myself. He takes this.

Njord showed me he is more than a fisherman, more than a mere god of boats on the waves. He is more than a captive diplomat and more than a father to great gods. There is a reason he and Nertha had twins, that these twins are gods of fertility. Njord, in his right and act of husbandry to the seas and lover of the earth, is a god of fertility.

I saw the wives of fishermen, their thighs and bellies washed with sea water, singing praises and prayers to Njord and other gods of the ocean. I saw them ask for his touch as they spread their legs to his waters. Their bellies swelled and they bathed them with ocean water for Njord's protection and maleness. When their waters broke and washed over them it was collected and given back to the ocean, water for water, in offering on the day they baptized their sons by the waves. They were blessed and their love for Njord was palpable.

I was shaken by the revelation, and by his intensity. Afterwards, Njord went back to his work. The full moon is a few nights away and the salmon are running, so he is busy. I gather myself and step onto the dock. Once I reach land, Hlin is there. She wraps me in her cloak as I kneel on the ground. My body is still swaying with the tide as Njord's water flows out of me, over my thighs and into the earth. I am clean and full of knowing.

Learning from Goodfather Njord
Raven Kaldera

Many years ago I took an intensive astrology course that gave me a number of really good tools for introspection. During some of the classes, we did long guided meditations in which we were encouraged to personify ten planets and five asteroids in our astrological birth charts. For those who don't know or care about astrology, think of it as a meditation where you are encouraged to imagine, meet, and talk to fifteen different aspects of yourself, sorted by titles like "the part that does romantic relationships", "the disciplinarian", "the wounded part", and so forth. As I went through the meditation, each aspect of myself congealed into a face, a body, and an environment. (Astrologically, their "home" was reflected in the "house" where that planet was located in the chart.) Some were male, some female, some shifted back and forth. Some were strong and powerful, others weak and hurting. I journaled heavily about this system of self-discovery, and over the years I found myself revisiting it again and again, checking in on my various aspects. It allowed me to figure out what parts of myself were complaining and in need of attention.

Probably the most pathetic one of all was the face that appeared when the meditation took me to "visit" the asteroid Ceres in my birth chart. For the non-astrologers, think "the part of yourself that nurtures others". Mine is in Cancer, unaspected, retrograde, and in the twelfth house; think "hard to access, and hidden most of the time". She appeared as a young woman, not even out of her teens, half-starved with dark circles around her eyes, living her life in a dark basement. I fled from the image, and besides writing about it in my journal, didn't look at it for a long time. Nurturing had never come easily or naturally to me, even when I was co-parenting a child. I did my best to be a kind and reasonable parent, and to remember to be affectionate even when it felt forced, but I constantly felt like I was moving blindly through a role I didn't feel, even as I loved my kid. My partners all knew that I'd willingly do things for them if asked, but caregiving just wasn't my thing.

I should backtrack and recount that I come from an extremely dysfunctional childhood with ill and violently physically abusive parents.

As the oldest child, I was expected to take on adult duties at a very young age, including caring for my younger sibling and sometimes even my parents themselves, and I hated it. I was forced to take over the cleaning of the house, even before I reached puberty; I deliberately screwed up and burned all attempts to force me to cook anything more complicated than toast, so that I couldn't be made to take that on as well. When I failed in my adult duties, which was often, I was brutally beaten. Caretaking, to me, was a painful prison. It was no surprise that my Ceres, my nurturing part, was hungry and shut up in the dark. I just didn't know what to do about it, because I couldn't seem to break those associations.

Nothing changed for decades until this year, when suddenly Njord showed up. I'd had visionary encounters with Him before, but I'd always been the one who approached respectfully and asked for advice or aid. This time He showed up while I was lying in bed, just barely awoken in the morning. "So," He said cheerfully. "It's time to do something about that poor abused Ceres of yours."

Earlier in the week, I'd been checking in on my various astrological "self-aspects" (with the exception of Ceres whom I'd ceased to visit because it was too depressing), and it had occurred to me that I'm a polytheist; were my different aspects drawn to my different Gods? Might they each be sort of henotheistic with one of the various deities in my personal Peanut Gallery? I visualized each aspect and asked the question. Some did, some didn't. My Saturn has always belonged to Hela; my Pluto was enamored of Shiva; my Neptune is devoted to Fenrir; my Venus reacts to Frey like a schoolgirl with a rock star; my Uranus tends to prefer elemental or plant or animal spirits. Some didn't have a deity-of-choice at all. But now here was Njord, speaking up for the imprisoned and least loved part. "I know all about astrology, you know," He said. "We sailors spend a lot of time staring at the sky. It was one of the few things Skadi and I bonded over— She stared at a lot of stars out on those frozen fields. Give me your Ceres," He said, "and I'll do some healing on those old wounds. Let him make Me his God and I'll do right by him."

"Him?" I said. "I thought she was a girl."

"At the moment," He said, "but you notice that she's not a grown woman, some Earth Mother-type with huge tits who pushes out babies?

The sort of woman you'd expect a nurturer to be? No, she was pushed into the job too young, without adequate feeding herself, which is why she's so ineffective. I think she'd do better as a man. He'd have more confidence. And we have to get him out of that dark basement."

"The twelfth house symbolizes places of confinement," I said. "I'm just going with the symbolism here."

Njord rolled His blue eyes. "Yes, it's confinement, and dark basements, and hospitals, and prisons ... but it's also dream, and fantasy, and the wellspring of poetry. *You* came up with that image, in your pain. I've got a better one. How about a ship, for example? You can't exactly leave a ship without drowning, once it's at sea, but it's a lot more comfortable than being locked in the basement. At least my ship is. There are stars, and sunset over the ocean, and camaraderie. Let me have him for my crew. He can sail off when you're not enacting that part of you, and come back to dock when someone in your life needs him." He paused. "And if he stays with me, I'll teach him how to be a good father, in a way you never got to understand."

I remembered how Njord is, in spite of His wanderings, very much a family man. He loves and is proud of His twin children, He dandles Freya's daughters on His knee, He cares about His wife at home and is honestly glad She has other consorts to keep Her company while He is away. He is the Goodfather in a very real sense, with experience in frith-making that is honed on a ship, where people can't leave and have to learn how to get along. Very much like a family, in its own way. What else could I do but agree? I needed some breakfast, because my blood sugar was falling, but I resolved to visit my poor incarcerated Ceres later in the day, and get her opinion of the matter.

It's funny how parts of one's self respond dramatically to the presence of Gods in ways that one's own personal efforts can't achieve. When I went down into that basement, my nurturing aspect had already shifted shape and was waiting expectantly. He was a bearded man in a knitted sweater and rubber boots, no longer young, but still thin and hollow-eyed. "I'm going to be the ship's cook," he told me. "Njord says if I work in the kitchen I'll never go hungry."

"Um, I don't really know how to cook," I said.

"*You* don't," he said. "Did you ever ask *me* about it?"

Later that week, I went into trance and formally brought this personified aspect of myself to Njord. I envisioned that the dark basement was in a shack within walking distance of the beach, and I brought him out and walked him to where Njord's ship was anchored—not a Viking ship, but a full-rigged Victorian number with mast after mast of billowing sails. He got into the rowboat and was brought to the ship, where Njord pierced his ear with a gold ring and showed him to the kitchen cauldrons. The surge of joy from deep inside me was so intense it made me cry. It still does, when I picture him standing on the deck of the ship, hair blowing, well-fed, handing out bowls of food to a laughing crew with a twinkle in his eye that he's recently learned from a certain old blue-eyed sailor.

The external-world manifestation of this internal shift was that I suddenly started cooking. Like, seriously cooking. OK, some of what I made wasn't exactly great, but you have to start somewhere, right? I've always been lucky to have partners who were decent-to-good cooks, so I never really had to learn how to do more than a few token dishes, but now the Goodfather had that part of me working the pots and cauldrons. I eventually surprised myself by making more elaborate dishes like chicken korma—I wonder what port they pulled into in order to inspire that?—including grinding all the spices for it. And, just today, baba ganoush! My partners were told about Njord's rescuing of my hesitant and newly-fledged nurturing self, and when I made a special snack for one of them and he said, "My compliments to the ship's chef," I got the feeling that he blushed and scuffed the deck with his boot.

Njord's rescue is just in time. My adult daughter is working on having a baby, and I'll be Grandpa. Maybe, the second generation around, I'll feel something besides confusion and resentment. Maybe Goodfather Njord will show me the way. After all, His children are the most beautiful ones in the Nine Worlds. With a resumé like that, how could we lose?

Njord Sails to Norse Lands
Heather Awen

When Daddy told us that we were leaving although I was young I was already ageless. Daddy and I had many meetings with the other Vanir including my brother Ingvi. All of the centuries traveling—the first Gods with the wheel, worshiped in the Balkans and Hungary, flowing to Austria with the copper route where we became eventually known as part of the Celts, Yngvi's tribe of North Sea Germans, our first interactions with the Saami as we learned new ways to build some of Daddy's boats and how to worship the bear, my own cults with the Baltic people, even the journeys across the Silk Road where I learned a magic that Odin would soon desire—we are the Gods of the wheel. We are the power that comes with a wagon.

But now we would be known for our master ships. It was Daddy's time to be chieftain and we gathered on our boat Vanaheim, waving goodbye to brothers and sisters, wondering about their fate. The deadly Cross we already knew had turned our cousins in Iberia into Saints, fairies, demons and folklore. The reason for our vote? Would we suffer the same fate? Rhiannon said she was the land and Arawn said he guarded the gateway to the dead of those tribes. Manawydan was there before any of us, native of the Isle of Man and so nobody was surprised that he quietly said no. Bran and Branwen were as loyal as could be to those people.

I could see a name threatening to rip them apart. The prophecy of Arthur. My heart burst watching Arawn become Gwyn ap Nudd and then a mere Lord of the Fairies to be erased by holy water—the Cross would rape Modron and bards would boast only about themselves, not the glory of the Gods. The Awenydd would forget their wild frenzies of prophecy that we had taught them and become mere slaves to paper telling stories that were far removed from their ecstatic beginnings.

It was too much for us to bear and so we boarded Vanaheim and made our way north. My dear brother absentmindedly commented on how the Angles and Jutes would bring him back to that island. Daddy saw his own future in the northern Isles when the Norwegians would flee South and the Vikings would first plunder and then settle in a place called Dublin, the center of cosmopolitan commerce. He would make many a trader both wealthy and worldly. I saw some of my own doom. In a land of fire and ice there would be a choice between the Cross and me. The people of the Cross had nothing that matched me and so I would live the longest as a Goddess.

Daddy knew where he was going; he had taken us there many times and we had kinfolk like Sif and her children UllR and Ullin waiting. Bright Hair of the Sun, the Great Queen Mother of the forest fertility twins, had already married one of the Gods traveling out of central Germany. They had lived south of us in the forests while we lived where the clay soil was so strong it took a plough of iron to allow us to bless the seeds.

Daddy was chieftain even as I was becoming a Queen. As the ocean spray wet my face Daddy called me by my ocean name, Mardoll. We sailed by the island where I was known as "the giver". Daddy had us yell out "We love you! We miss you!" to his sister, our mother, Nerthus when we passed her island. As the fog rose Daddy told us that Mother was saying hello, engulfing us in her veil.

Heimdall became anxious to see his own mothers, the nine that it took to satisfy Daddy. Like everyone in our family Daddy was known for his sexual stamina and when he could, he would take my half brother and visit the nine wave sisters.

"You know," said Heimdall, his golden teeth flashing, something Daddy gave Heimdall when he tried too young to surf the waves and wiped out, "Our Gaelic cousins would say we have been exiled beyond the ninth wave." And he gave a grin that almost blinded me. "For me I am coming back over the ninth wave, my mothers, so this will be my home."

I nodded, knowing that if an exile washed back to land alive the humans understood that we Gods did not want that person dead and disowned. For Heimdall, who was born from nine pearls of Daddy's semen taken within the nine daughters of Aegir and Ran, in many ways this would be his first time coming home. I knew that he would stay and I knew that he would be loyal to that place until the end of time, even if it meant his death while Vanaheim lived on.

My brother, already strong and perfect from ages of selected cross-fertilization, stood like a man by Daddy. Daddy was still much taller, needing those long arms for grabbing ropes and nets, but my brother was wider.

"What will we do when we arrive?" He asked.

"What we did before," Daddy said staring off to the horizon. "We will make friends with the Gods and trade knowledge. If the Saami who did not even speak our language could be such gracious hosts and teach us of their magic and the technology needed to survive when we arrived long ago, I'm sure that our young German cousins will remember us. After all, the Saxons have already begun befriending the remaining tribes of the people of Yngvi. They will be brothers and sisters soon. The worship of the remaining German tribes will mix and we will have a new family."

Ingvi looked worried. Like Daddy he stared into the horizon, but I could tell he wasn't looking at the ocean. He was looking at the future.

"What if my German siblings have changed? The ones that stayed destroyed the crumbling Empire, but they took the Cross. What if having their people forced to a new religion has made them afraid of other Gods? Maybe those natives have become paranoid." His pupils were dilated. "Their grief must be great. I do not think they will trust us."

Daddy kept his eyes focused on that one spot on the horizon and said, "If they do not remember the days of Mannus, the one who rebirthed the world from Tuisto to make us Germans, and the brotherhood that you yourself have with them, Golden Drink will announce that she comes with powerful brothers and sisters to share the sacred Mead."

Gullveig looked up from the deck where she was sitting. She was sturdy, with the hair the color of rich soil that my brother loved. Perhaps it reminded him of our mother. He was always her Golden Boy.

Nothing seemed to bother Gullveig. Where I was adventurous, always getting off the wagons and the ships, she was content to sit, using her gifts to look backwards and root herself in the deepest of our family magic. I knew she knew everything but the ways of men. Daddy had his reasons for choosing her, although I had wanted to be the first. Daddy said my temperament was not appropriate for this event. Ingvi had laughed and said, "She would fuck them to death." I stood to play wrestle in mock anger but his arms held me and I kissed him.

I said the cruel thing only siblings will dare say. "Remember, brother, that you are the one who dies every year." I knew it wasn't good to joke about death but it was springtime and we were in love and my mother's deadly scythe would not come for months.

"Quiet, the two of you." Daddy held a Sunstone, catching a glimpse of Sif's hair. "We are soon to land."

Sometimes I forgot how commanding my father was. With my Sight I knew, like all of us on that ship, that we would have to fight in order to dock our boat to the new World Tree in front of us. Then it would be the business of my brother and myself to make Vanaheim blossom again into abundant lands with the finest sheep and the strongest grains. I knew this but doubted if Gullveig, the sedate Goddess of mead, so used to pleasant outcomes, understood what was to happen.

Of course I shouldn't have worried. Gullveig had been sitting in her own cocoon. When we landed and she arrived at the walled city of Asgard, mead in hand, knocking at the door, we prepared for the inevitable. Daddy had thick leathers covering his body and his face, sword in hand, plus a spear that they never would have seen because it was made for harpooning fish. As deadly as it was for the cattle of the ocean, it was twice as deadly for the man who was hooked. Even Ran herself fled from its blade.

When I heard my beloved Gullveig scream, I was ready to blow down the walls with Daddy. I have a combination of his weather magic and my skills of destruction, which many forget I have, but like my mother before me I am as much a part of death as I am fertility. I am the Van Norn who cuts your thread on the battlefield.

Odin's spear barely had left his hand before Daddy reached up and grabbed it. His face contorted, making what could be seen under the leather look cruel. Odin's weapon had the magic to scatter enemies, but our army took the strength of a thousand wild boars and stormed the field. First Daddy, enraged, snapped the spear in half, and then we ran past the fallen wall.

The battle was easy enough once we took stock of the enemy. Odin didn't have the pure fury that he did in the German woods when his life was lived in the fastest winds, the screams of the storm. He had had to temper those, years wandering among humans learning their ways. He found he enjoyed finding knowledge, which became his new passion unless war kept him from this great, new love. A dead volva, one of our own, would tell him more than he should have wanted to hear. That would be his biggest regret, not stopping his questions and thus spending his life preparing for a war he knew would lose. Later he would counsel humans not to be overwise.

In battle he combined the storm's fury with his growing education about leadership and power. This was after the one we now called Tyr, a great battle commander when fighting other Germans who shared the same sense of honor, stepped down when the enemies became the ruthless Romans and Huns. Now Tyr judged the internal battles of the folk. I noted his hand was missing. Their thunderer was temporarily distracted by the crafty, practical Sif, who knew all our mind-altering magics but never told her husband's people. Loki watched with great interest from afar to see who would win. His family, even his children, of Gods had already been brutalized by the Aesir and yet he kept his brotherhood to Odin. My brother was right. These German siblings feared the original Gods of these winter-dark lands.

Daddy was laughing when they begged for truce. So was I, bloodlust running through my veins, which is why the Aesir would make me their priestess, the woman who sacrificed. I fed the blood to the land as did my brother and my father because these people did not know any fertility magic. They knew how to sacrifice for killing in war, but not how to bring scorched land back to life. My brother and I would keep the fields and flocks full as Daddy would call the herring to the nets. All we needed was a knife.

Yet we suddenly learned the one who truly knew about life, so much that she couldn't die, was Gullveig. Now we understood for what she had been preparing all these eons.

My brother was the one who touched my arm and pointed. Just like how the best smiths knew to melt down gold three times to make it the most pure, my beloved Gullveig had known from her gift of prophecy that fire would be the strategy of the Aesir. And she took full advantage of it.

She who used to carry the sacred Mead as a way of making peace had been ripped apart by their swords and spears. What she later would call the dross fell to the ground and when the fires came she let herself be burned, each time growing stronger, growing brighter, growing in power beyond any of our imagined dreams. She lived, the collective magic of our history running through her veins.

"You have lost, little men," she said with the largest smile I'd ever seen on her face. "You have unleashed your biggest fear and I am happy to be her." She was strong and she was shining like pure gold. In her hand was half of the shaft from Odin's magic spear, which she ran her fingers across, turning it into a beautiful jewel-encrusted staff.

Ingvi whispered to me, "Do you know who she is?"

I said, "More like *what* she is." For I am one, too, but my royal duties kept me from wandering with the staff. The Heids may pray to me but I was not to be a volva. Not like that.

We watched her turn to us, tall like Daddy, hair scorched pale yellow, dressed in the finest traveling clothes like she was ready to take to the trail, but to where?

Daddy embraced her and keeping her under one strong arm announced, "Today the people are blessed because the women of this land have their own Heid." He kissed her cheek and they locked eyes for a moment. "I thought I had sent you to your death doom but it is a golden doom indeed." They laughed and my eyes filled with tears of happiness.

Odin wanted to discuss hostages. "The gold one," he said. He pointed at Gullveig Heid.

She threw back her head and smiled shaking her head slowly. First she walked to me and gave me a strong hug, whispering in my ear "I will always keep our magic going; it cannot die." Then she went to my brother doing the same, but what she said I did not hear. He would tell me later.

Past Tyr, past Thor, she glided still smiling and shaking her head, but her stare was fixed on the one to soon lose an eye after we decapitated his wisest one, one more from Loki's kin than the Aesir's. Untouchable, she kissed Sif and kept moving. Thor was too caught in battle rage to notice but Loki did.

All eyes were locked on her as she stepped over the rubble, paused listening to the winds, and then turned north. The last thing we heard her say was "Always remember where the sky has been nailed. The Finns will remind you, but that was the first thing the Saami taught us."

Daddy said, "She could navigate the seas. Now she will train women in navigating wyrd. This land is already blessed by us."

Then he turned to Odin. "You have lost the strongest of us all, fury man. As chieftain of the Vanir, I offer myself in her stead. Your men will need a God of sailing to grow wealthy in trade. The humans of the rocky land Norway will starve without my skill with fish. You have none to ride the waves safely above Ran."

Odin slightly nodded. Those humans in the west were so poor they could not make offerings. Without offerings, how could the Gods help? Especially without a God who could help. Thor's rains brought them ice instead and Odin could no longer continue to favor one region than another in war to bring them wealth when the spoils had grown so scarce.

Ingvi, so used to being sacrificed for the greater good, spoke next. "You may have me, and need me you will, for I am God of food. Every farmer will know my name: Lord." I had never heard him use that title. They were smart, making themselves indispensable.

"Lord?" asked an angry Thor. "I am to call you Lord? I already help the farmers."

"You are not the wealth of the seed. You cannot bless the horses mating. I have the fertility of ten thousand Gods and more. And yes, you will call me by my name Frey. Who will feed your warriors, Odin?"

I smiled at my lover's bravery. Odin had already agreed.

Odin pointed to me. "Her. She knows that magic."

Daddy said, "We agreed to two hostages each. And now my daughter is Lady of Vanaheim." I silently applauded Daddy's wisdom. "However, she is ... close with her brother. Perhaps when she visits, if you have something to offer, she would teach you the women's magic."

Loki said, "My blood brother always has something to offer women with wisdom he wants. Although it is no magic to seduce and use a maiden, he makes it appear so."

I ignored him, sensing that he wanted the power too, but had nothing to bargain for it. To Odin I said, "Do you really wish to know the dread skills of nercomancy?" Watching his hungry eyes, I sold it. I sold him the words with which I could make my trade. "That magic which controls the psyches of living and dead? Prophecies that prepare a man for death and a woman for motherhood?" I nodded to Frigga. "Ones that can actually be shared like a harlot shares her love?"

"You already know I do, woman. What would you take in trade?"

I spoke clearly. "The first choice of the fallen warriors."

Odin agreed before Tyr could stop him.

That's how Daddy brought our people to the tree of now nine worlds and ensured we'd always have the power of Gods.

Building Bridges
Brandon E. Hardy

Back in 2012, I received my first introduction to modern Pagan practice. I had reached out to a spiritual teacher a few months before this point and was doing small tasks for him as we got to know each other. As I was living closer to the coast at that point, he asked me to scout the nearby Boston harbor for a good place to have a ritual for the newest god-pole addition to his land. (Or, to be more faithful to his exact words, "a place near ships to dunk a log and sing.")

It ended up being far easier than I had feared to find a good place and describe where it was, but when the ritual came around a week or so later, it ended up being one of those days for me. You know, one of *those*. Not only did I sleep through my alarm as all classic "those days" start, but I found myself lost looking for the very place I had described in an email only days before. I eventually sat down in defeat against some concrete building, holding my cell phone that had just reached the same answering machine for the third time while watching the boats go by. There was no call back until the ritual was well over (reasonably), so I only ended up loitering around the wet log with a smattering of people I didn't really know, but it was nice enough.

Then the next high holiday rolled around and the god-pole was to be placed in the ground. I didn't quite know what the right thing to do was at that point, so I found myself sitting by an unlit bonfire with a member of the group who didn't feel moved to join in the dedication. While trying to make small talk, I experienced something I have since learned this group was affectionately infamous for: enthusiastic pronunciation correction.

"So, that pole is going in for... Nuh-johrd?"

"*Njord*."

We chatted some more until the singing at the far end of the field wrapped up, then the festivities continued along. The N'whatever god mostly slipped from my mind amid the flood of information that is Paganism 101. Months later I was heading down to the ritual field by myself, I think to collect something that had been forgotten. I can say for sure it was during the height of summer, though, because I clearly remember clipping up my hair as far away from my sweaty neck as possible in a sadly futile act of desperation. At some point I happened to glance across the field where that pole with all the fishing nets on it had been firmly planted a few months previously, and it was like a lightning bolt shot down my body to strike me between the legs. And it was a very friendly lightning bolt. I looked away with what I feel was an appropriate amount of shock and hurriedly continued about my business. I will admit that I did glance over again a couple more times, though honestly it was probably a good five or ten more times. I eventually tried pointedly looking at other poles and thinking of other things when I looked back to Him, yet the only thing that seemed to cause this notable reaction was whether or not I was looking at that one particular carved log.

But that was crazy, and I was obviously being crazy, and I had a sizable folder of official documents about my crazy saying that I had a solid and reliable history of being crazy, so I decided with great pride in my self-awareness to simply take that as one more crazy to disregard and never let grace the light of day. And I did a really wonderful job of that ... until my teacher said something off-hand and remarkably poignant three months later that caused my eyes to go wide and mild panic to set in. I talked to him about that hot summer day (probably with more disclaimers than actual content) and there were some bluntly forthright Tarot cards thrown down, all followed by many more months of confusion, anxious indecision, and a completely unreasonable amount of sailor-related motifs everywhere I turned.

Now, over five years later, I find myself sitting at my laptop organizing a number of submissions for a devotional to this deity who has become a part of my life to the point that I carry His mark permanently on my flesh. Yet what keeps coming to mind when I try to add my part is how confused and reluctant I was to pursue Him in the beginning. More than anything it was simply wondering, why? He was first explained to me as a Deity of Sailors and Fishermen. At that point I had a long-held aversion to sailing, and when a childhood friendship with a lobster went horribly wrong, that aversion firmly included fishing. So why would Njord think there could be any devotional affinity between us?

Yet the more I read and learned about Him, the more I understood. So when I was called to end my twenty-one-year streak of being a vegetarian, He and His son Frey were there, offering Their warm smiles to the child in me who still couldn't quite let go. When therapy took a turn for some long unresolved issues, He offered to be the Good Father who held me and slowly drew the poison out of the phrase "don't rock the boat". And when I asked why I had always seemed to get laid far more often when I drank a lot of rum, He also kindly cleared up the reasons for that particular blessing in my life.

But even with all the ways I found myself drawn to Him and what He offered, there was a big, overarching theme of His that made things clear: He's a peacemaker between warring sides, and the very act of having anything to do with me is a fulfillment of that role. That's because I'm a Christian.

I'm not going to discuss here how that part of my spirituality works itself out—enough Christians have taken up space reserved for Pagan deity, often in a painfully literal way — so let's just take it on good faith that I'm first and foremost about the big J.C. and that he was the one who got me into polytheism to begin with. So as I was finding my footing in places where Christians don't have the best history of relations (to put it mildly), it seems reasonable that this Pagan God of truces and frith-making would be the first one I got to know.

From what I can tell, these two peacemakers have been forming the foundations for this bridge for a while now, and its construction is a primary focus of my devotional practice. In a literal representation of this (because I'm a bit of an altar enthusiast), Jesus' altar takes up most of the space around the head of my bed, while the foot is surrounded by Njord and His family. Pictures of lighthouses held aloft by smooth metal pushpins span the slanted ceiling between Them. I sometimes lie there thinking about the things They share—a fondness for fishermen, a touch that calms the waters around Them, noteworthy lore about women and Their feet, a desire for peace strong enough to inspire the sacrifice of a king—and wonder if these bits of common ground are capable of supporting a bridge as heavy as the one between Them would be. Could They truly sit together, trading these tales, clinking a bottle of rum against a bottle of wine in the spirit of brotherhood, and have that be the foundation of a bridge that would span millennia of hate and bloodshed?

Then sometimes the self-reflection shoulders its way in and I look at those places in my life where I see no way to make peace; where there's obviously not enough usable common ground for me to consider even trying for a rope bridge. Maybe there was not enough flat, solid space between the mounds of anger ... at least anywhere that I would care to look. And yet there They are, sitting at either end of me, the seemingly unspannable distance decorated with secondhand posters and calendar cutouts tacked up in celebration of where They can both find joy. If They find those small bits of frith that form in Their wake worth the effort, then perhaps those bridges I have been avoiding aren't completely impossible. Even if they can't be built on either side just yet, maybe there are small things I can do to create a space where the bridge could take shape. And Njord is just the God to know how to make it happen.

Because as that famous Rumi saying doesn't quite go: Out beyond the ideas of wrong-doing and right-doing there is a bridge. Quite a few of them, in fact. And I'm guessing that by them there will be a blue-eyed sailor with a deep laugh and a wide grin welcoming us with open arms to rejoice in His handiwork.

Njord the Cold-Hearted Business Man
Heather Awen

I am Njord
Whose name is synonymous with risk.
Every person who has been on the sea has felt my fear.
No one gets on the boat
Without good reason.
Vietnamese boat people,
Vikings of raid to trade,
Run away from home
Join the Navy.
No one gets on the boat without good reason.
My cities conquered seas
Dominating the land from ports,
All Noatun to me.
Who had the Irish Sea
Was made King by me
And even if the commerce was slavery
No one gets on the boat without good reason,
Even if the reason is nothing more than money.
Pray to me, venture capitalist
And libertarian who wants to hold your power in place
At the top of the criminal food chain,
I expect you on the boat
But don't expect the boat to be kind.
The Anglo-Saxon rune poem knew me best-
A sea voyage for which many
Are not prepared.
They will die,
You will die
If you don't stand firm on the soil of my wife
And leave my ships behind.

I am Njord
And Dublin to York was my capitol.
Those waves, that rough water,
Which allowed Ireland her first cities.
My Norwegian worshippers
Balking at a centralized nation
Arrived in Gaelic lands,
Bringing old Gods back
And building streets that still hide under Dublin.
No need to go deeper into the land.
Artisans fill my ports
With the wealth of many lands.
In Dublin you heard the many languages
Required for wealth
The wealth of diversity
And you'll see me just as happy in
New Orleans
As I am in the Hebrides.

A shipyard is shipyard
Even when the fish are poisoned
And birds covered in oil.
The Anglo-Saxon rune poem never says
Water nourishes,
Only that the ocean will terrify those unready
Like you.
A steadier income to you on land
For the ocean's get-rich-quick-scheme members
All live in broken oak villages under the waves
And Ran can reach them from where they steer
In corporate board rooms
And she's bored with silver coins.

I am Njord
The God of wealth

And as such the Diar of the Aesir Gods
With my son,
The other wealthy one.
We are the sacrificial Priests
Just like in Iceland
How by mere financial strength
A man performed the sacrifices
That blessed the people.
Money equalled Priest
And do you still believe that?
(The Aesir didn't understand our ways,
So think before you confine me by their bound culture.)

I am Njord
God of wind
Remembered in the land of fire and ice
By a Gaelic name Diar,
One never shared with an Aes.
As the land became less hospitable
With clear cut trees
Forcing people on the boat
To Vinland, seeking lumber,
My wife Nerthus stayed with her clay bogs
Made fertile only with an iron plough shaping her,
Scars she covers with a veil.

I am Njord
And once my name had meaning,
"Power" just like my wife Nerthus.
Neart mara dhuit,
Neart talamh dhuit,
Neart nèimhe.[1]

---

[1] *Carmina Gadelica*, Alexander Carmichael.

[Power of sea be with you,
Power of land be with you,
Power of sky.]

I am Njord
And not everyone who gets on the boat
Survives.
Those filled with either desperation or greed
Cry out to me,
King of the Van,
Diar, Gaelic God of sacrificial Priest
Power of wind, controlling sea and fire
As they take the risk
Coerced or Free Will.
Some will found kingdoms
And many others will wreck upon the reefs.
Steal and sell is still
Breaching boats and making slaves out of the unlucky.

I am Njord
And what has been forgotten
Is that I own the wealth
And it shifts
As my wind blows.

All Hands On Deck: Devotional and Ritual Practices

Ship Herd
Michaela Macha

The gulls bring word of you who widely fares
to tell the fishes where to find our net;
they've come from Noatun to claim their shares,
like you at home both in the dry and wet.
Within your waters play the Sisters Nine
who bask in rising Sunna's brilliant blush,
as waves frolic in the golden shine
until the purple nightfall's gentle hush.
O tranquil Lord of seven surging seas,
send wind to fill our sails, and grant us all
to pass to our ports with grace and ease
over the depths of Ran's and Aegir's Hall.
And let us in the midst of storms be stout,
firm as an anchor in the shifting sands,
that change and stay the same, tide in, tide out,
beneath your briny realm that bounds the lands.

Charms for Njord
Geordie Ingerson

(All material by Geordie Ingerson is excerpted with permission from the book Ingvi's Blessing: Prayers and Charms for Field and Farm, *Asphodel Press 2012.)*

For a Wooden Boat

Hail to the trees that gave their lives
And chose to adventure on the water with me,
May you bear me up bravely on the waves.
Hail to the Fisher-King, Goodfather Njord,
Lord of billowing white sails, lord of churning white wakes,
Saviour of mariners for many centuries,
Patron of poor fishermen who plumb the depths,
Blessing of every small boat on a river,
Bless this sea-steed that will bear me
Over the blue hills, down the blue roads,
Across the blue fields, through your silver herds.
Let her never sink, let her never buck,
Make her sure-footed as a fine mare
And tight as a locked cottage.
Bless my sail, my rudder, my masts,
Bless fore and aft, port and starboard.
Bless my boat, Vanaheim's King,
With your gentle, skilful hands.

For a Fishing-Net

Goodfather Njord, with knot and needle
I make this net to fish your waters,
Weight it well and fill it full
Of shining treasure tailed and finned.

For a Fishing-Float

The glass balls that are used to float nets are known as "Njord's Eyes" among my Vanic friends, and cork floats are "Njord's Fingerbones". Here are two versions of a charm to bless them before lowering the net into the water.

Gentle gaze the Fish-King's eyes,
High in the water and turn to the sky.

Gentle grasp the Fish-King's hands,
Haul up my nets from wave to sand.

For A Fishing-Rod

Shepherd of Fishes, favour me.
I am a man sensible and strong
Of moral fibre and of worthy will,
Well I merit your gifts, so send
Silver-scaled supper to my line,
O Goodfather Njord who knows my need.

A Prayer for the Fishers of Lakes
Sarenth Odinsson

May the fish be plentiful,
May the waters be clean,
May the rivers and streams be clear.

May the poles be strong,
May the bait be seductive,
May the lines be free of tangles.

May the catch be good,
May the day be blessed,
May Njord guide and protect.

Devotional Ritual for Njord
Galina Krasskova

This ritual is a little different. It's not meant to be done regularly; in fact, depending where you live, it can take some preparation. The purpose of this ritual is to serve as a devotional rite honoring the God Njord, by taking His image (be it a carving, a statue, a laminated picture) to the ocean. As early as the writings of Tacitus, the use of processions honoring Vanic Gods has been attested to in lore.[9] So for this ritual, the idea is to carry your statue or image of Njord to the ocean where it can be anointed with seawater.

This is a very open-ended ritual. It can be as simple or elaborate as you wish. Choose the music that you will play in the car with Njord in mind. Dress in colors that you associate with Him. Prepare food or offerings that can be given to Him on the beach. Display the God-image proudly in your car (which admittedly can take some doing). Begin by offering the following prayer:

Father Njord,
Warlord of the Vanir,
Hostage of Peace,
Diplomat,
Sea-farer
Master of Ships
Lord of the boat-yard.
I hail You.

Father of Freya,
Father of Frey,
Husband of Nerthus,
Husband of Skadhi,
Peaceloving Master of Noatun

---

[9] Nerthus ritual, *Germania*, chapter 40.

May this offering be pleasing to You,
Oh my Lord.

    Proceed onward to the ocean. Once there, take the image of Njord to the shoreline and allow the water to flow over it—holding on carefully so it isn't gifted to the sea itself! Then set out the offerings and spend as much time as you wish in communion with Njord. Make sure the offerings are organic and biodegradable so that they can be left on the beach by the water's edge. Best of all, make it something the seagulls will enjoy.

    Return home, displaying Njord's image mindfully and prayerfully and once home, return it to its altar knowing that the ritual has ended.

Offerings to Njord
Raven Kaldera

Njord is the fisherman's God, and as such he is very concerned with the health of the oceans. For him, however, while pollution is definitely a problem, his main concern is the overfishing of the seas due to industrial fisheries. The oceans are running out of fish at a fast rate, and this is a terrible thing to him. Njord would like to see industrial fisheries banned and fishing returned to small fishermen, especially small fishing families - much as his son Frey prefers small family farms over huge industrial agribusiness farms and feedlots. The new term on the horizon is "artisanal fishermen", for the smaller fishing boats who do it the old-fashioned way, without dangerous dragnets and enormous waste of fish. These are Njord's people, and to support them is to honor him.

Some suggestions might be:

- Write to Congress about ocean acidification concerns and overfishing. Encourage them to cut all subsidies for industrial fisheries and eventually ban those. At the least, ask them to ban bottom trawling and destructive fishing. Ask them to ban offshore drilling—we can't guarantee that the BP accident won't happen again. Ask them to subsidize, instead, artisanal fishing boats and sustainable fish farming companies.

- Write to your trade minister and ask them to pressure the UN to outlaw "flags of convenience", which allow ships from industrialized nations to fly the flags of smaller, poorer countries who agree to look the other way on illegal overfishing, catching waste, boundary violations, and pollution.

- Write to your government and ask them to set aside more offshore areas to be "preserves" where no fishing can happen—we need some places where the fish stocks can recover and be breeding grounds for the rest of the oceans. Ask them to pressure the UN into pushing this agenda.

- Recruit your local seafood restaurateur or market owner to do the same - he can't afford to run out of fish either.

- Eat sustainably caught fish, and encourage your friends and family to do the same. The Monterey Bay Aquarium Seafood Watch pamphlet is a good resource for this. Download a batch and distribute them. Voting with your wallet is the best way to go.

- Contact local restaurants and ask them not to use "red-list" seafood. Eat at restaurants that serve sustainable fish. Fish2Fork is a good organization to check for this.

- Don't eat bluefin tuna, and contact sushi places and ask them not to use it either.

- Don't buy coral jewelry - we're killing the reefs fast enough as it is, and they are needed to nurture fish birthing grounds.

- Put in a volunteer stint as a bycatch observer aboard a fishing vessel. These volunteers make sure that "bycatch" fish—meaning any fish that the boat can't or isn't interested in selling, which can be up to 75% of any given catch—are actually thrown back alive and not just killed. When you're there, you're a direct agent of Njord.

- If you live within driving distance of the ocean, support local artisanal fishermen. See if it's possible to buy directly from any of them instead of going through middlemen. See if you can organize a CSA (Community Supported Agriculture) share program among local fishermen and your friends who want to eat sustainable fish.

- Find out about the difference between sustainable and unsustainable aquaculture, and support (through buying and eating) the sustainable variety. RAS (recirculating aquaculture systems) is the most sustainable sort; find out where those industries are and buy from them (and push restaurants to do the same). The same "feedlot" issues that Njord's son Frey abhors on land are no better when they are applied in the waters.

- Write to the FDA and ask them to ban the importation of fish farmed with quinolones and other harmful antibiotics.

- If you own a boat, join Sailors for the Sea, which is an organization for recreational boaters who want to help preserve the oceans. If you live near a pier, leaflet recreational boats with their info (or give it to anyone with a boat in their front yard).

- Support organizations like the Gulf Fishermen's Association, which is trying to ensure a future for small fishermen who are being put out of business by industrial fishing.

- Donate time or resources to the American Oceans Campaign (Oceana.org) and the World Forum of Fishermen and Fish Workers (working to support sustainable fishing and small family fisheries).

Prayer to Njord for Direction
Taji Michihili

O Lord of the Sextant and Compass
Whose eye is the ship's wheel
Whose beckon is the sail filling with wind
Proud and erect like the mainmast
I am lost in a storm and cannot see
Stars, tides, or any landfall at all.
Mist surrounds me, and I fear running aground
On the rocks of failure, on the sandbars of disaster,
On the lonely island beach of apathy.
Lighthouse Lord, Savior of Sailors,
I would sail my life with confidence,
Knowing how to reach every one of my goals,
Or at least as many as are good for me,
And you would know that better than I.
Show me the coastline of manifestation
And patiently draw me the map to its shore,
O Njord who loves the wheeling gulls that cry.
Bring me safe to harbor with your shining light
High on the crag above the treacherous stones,
And let the ship that is my life not sink,
Nor founder on all the errors I claim,
Ruefully, as my ever-churning wake.
Hail King of Vanaheim who knows when to speak
And when to keep silent, Diplomacy's Sovereign,
O God who always knows where he may be floating.

Njord's Recipe: Salmon Baked in a Salt Dome
Seawalker

Note: This recipe is made with Alaskan wild-caught salmon, a fish that migrates from salt to fresh water every year. However, any good-sized fish can be substituted. The ideal would be a fish that you caught yourself, though.

- 1 wild-caught Alaska salmon
- 4 egg whites
- ½ cup water
- 2 3-lb. boxes of salt
- Handful of herbs—parsley, marjoram, what you have on hand
- 1 fennel bulb (with stem), quartered
- Several sprigs thyme
- Pan lined with tinfoil, big enough for the fish to lay flat

Rinse fish inside and out with cold water, drain and wipe dry, and stuff with herbs. You can rub it with a bit of olive oil and lemon juice and sprinkle more herbs on the outside if you like, but it shouldn't drip much.

Pour one box of salt into a large bowl, add egg whites and water, then the second box of salt. Use your hands to work the mixture to a mortar-like consistency, and then lay down a ½" layer for the fish with a 1-inch clearance on all sides. Lay the fish on this bed and pile the remainder of the salt mortar on top, making a smooth dome that completely encases the fish.

Cook for between 30 and 45 minutes depending on your oven, at around 450 degrees. It's hard to check for doneness, because you don't want to mess up the dome. Some people like to use one of those instant-read thermometers stuck periodically into a hole in the dome. The ideal would be getting the inside to 130 degrees, but if you're doing this over a campfire, you might want to leave the tail sticking out and use it as a way to test (with a small sharp knife) if the inside is done.

Opening the salt dome can be done at the table, with a hammer and a great flourish to break the dome. Lift off the slabs of salt, brush off the fish, and either carve it or let your guests hack into it themselves. If you want to be impressive, slit it and lift the skeleton out entirely. If it's cooked enough, it should come right out. This is an excellent Njord's Blot main dish.

Rite of Admiration to Njord
Rev Angela Kunschmann

This rite is written for the solitary practitioner. It can easily be altered for a group as you see fit. Wear what you feel most comfortable in or are called to wear.

This rite should be conducted near a moving body of water: ocean, river, creek, or even a lake. If no moving body of water is at your ready, please do use a large bowl of water in a wide open mouthed container.

Items needed:
- Small table for altar
- Cloths in light blue and green
- Lanterns
- Tealights
- Seashells and rocks
- Pictures of sailboats and large ships
- Drawing, picture, or statue of Njord
- Small container for water
- Chalice with vodka
- Dark hearty bread
- Incense or sage
- Salt water for anointing

Altar: Keep it simple. Light blue and green cloths that resemble the sea would be ideal, as are lanterns with tea lights inside. Include any seashells or rocks from the nearby body of water. Do collect a small amount of water from said body of water as well. Offerings of vodka and some hearty bread would be best. Pictures of sailboats and large ships as well as of Njord himself should also be on the altar. No worries about placement; do what feels right.

Smudge lightly with your favorite incense or some sage. Anoint with some salt water and envision Njord kissing you lightly on the forehead as you anoint.

Stand in the north (barefoot if you are able). Feel the earth beneath your feet. Imagine that tiny roots are growing out of your feet and down into the ground, anchoring you and keeping you grounded.

Stand in the east. Feel the breeze run all around you. Let it bring you images of inspiration. Let it be the power behind your voice. Remember that the east brings you a new day, every day.

Stand in the south. Feel the sun on your face. Feel the passion arise within, that passion to be the best person you can possibly be. This is where ideas are born, let them flow into you.

Stand in the west. If you are able, dip your toes into the water. Let the west wash over you and cleanse you.

Stand in the center and say:

Hail Njord,
Father of Frey and Freyja,
Lord of the Ships,
Master of the Seas,
I welcome you into this time and space.
May you join me as I bring offerings of adoration to you!

Stand at the altar. Hold the chalice of vodka and say:

Hail Njord,
Father of the Seas!
I offer this Vodka to you.
You show us to stand firm,
To hold our own until we reach the shore.
May this drink be as smooth as the calm sea
And light a fire in my belly.
Hail Njord!

Take a drink, pour the rest into the body of water or the ground. Hold the dark bread and say:

Hail Njord!
Master of the Ships!
I offer this bread to you.
You show us how to reap the rewards of our hard work.
May this bread be as rewarding and filling.
Hail Njord!

Take a bite, leave the rest for the birds and other animals in the area. Stand in the center and say:

Hail Njord!
I offer you nothing but praise and admiration.
You who protect us on the rocky waters of life.
You who provide riches for us when we work hard for ourselves.
You who show us how to be peace loving and diplomatic.
May my offerings, praise, and admiration be received well.
Hail Njord!

Turn to the west and dip your toes in the water if you are able. Think of swimming in cool lakes, sitting in a warm tub, and all manner of water that cleanses you.

Turn to the south and revisit with that warm sun. Remember those ideas you had that perhaps you haven't embarked on. Now is the time to reconsider and reignite those passions.

Turn to the east and feel the breeze around your face. Imagine gusty winds pushing a sailboat. Carrying the smell of salt water to many lands. This is your new day.

Turn to the north and remember the rooted feeling. Pull your roots back up, but keep some of them peeping out of your toes, just so that you stay grounded for the rest of the day.

Navigating by the Stars
Geordie Ingerson

When you are navigating by the stars, especially on water—but really, it will do anywhere you can see the ocean of stars—say this prayer to keep you safe:

> As the ocean of stars turns above
> So the ocean of wave turns below.
> Father Njord, help me find the one by the other,
> Make my eyes sure in the darkness,
> Make my hand sure on the rudder,
> Lead me safe home again.

Prayer to Njord
Galina Krasskova

Hail to Njord, Master of Ships!
Hail to Njord, Lord of Vanaheim!
Hail to Njord, loving Husband!
Hail to Njord, devoted Father!
God of temperance and even-handed care,
Who nourishes all within His hall,
Nourish our hearts, and minds and spirits,
That we may love You better and more deeply,
As the ocean loves the sand
And the sand hungers for the tide.

Invocation to Njord
Seawalker

(Excerpted from The Pagan Book of Hours)

When using this for daily prayer, I found this invocation can also be a protection and blessing spell using the Western 7 chakra system. With the author's permission, I added optional italicized instructions, with the standard descriptions of where most people can find these chakras, in case others wish to use it this way. -Brandon E. Hardy

(Face North, then rest your dominant hand on your crown chakra on the top of your head.)

Hail, Njord, Lord of the Surface of the Sea!

(Move your hand to your root chakra by your groin.)

Hail, Sailor's Watcher,
Lord of Ships upon the waters.

(Hold your hand out in front of you, palm facing North.)

Blessed you are in the prow,
Where you lead us forward to our goals.

(Hold your hand behind your head, palm facing South as best as you are able.)

Blessed you are in the stern,
Where you guard our wake
From the monsters of the Deep.

(Put your palm facing West, as if touching the inner wall of a ship.)

Blessed you are on the port,

Where your keen eyes search the horizon.

(Put your palm facing East, as if now touching the opposite wall.)

Blessed you are on the starboard,
Where you guide us by the stars.

(Touch your third eye chakra in the middle of your forehead.)

Blessed you are on the high mast,
Where you stand tall with far vision.

(Touch your throat chakra just above the hollow of your throat.)

Blessed you are in the sails,
Which you fill with billowing winds.

(Touch your solar plexus chakra right below the center of your ribcage.)

Blessed you are at the rudder,
Where you skillfully outrun all storms.

(Touch your heart charka in the center of your chest.)

Blessed you are at the nets,
Where the fish come by the thousands
Into our hands.

(Put both hands folded over your sacral chakra in your lower abdomen.)

Blessed you are below-decks,
Where you rock us gently to sleep
On the waves of certainty,
Knowing that the farthest shore
Will soon be under our feet.

(Raise your hands up, then put your palms together in front of you, your fingers upright as if they were sails on a small boat.

Hail Njord, Lord of Ships,
Guide our souls safely across the waters.

(Blow some wind into the "sails" of your small boat and move it away from you until your hands separate.)

A Prayer for a Strong Ship
Sarenth Odinsson

May the frame be strong and flexible,
May the engine be powerful and measured,
May the prow cut swift through the waters.

May the deck be sturdy and resolute,
May the hold be solid and sealed,
May the cargo be safe and secure.

Bless this ship, O Ship-builder,
May this vessel be strong,
May its crew be skilled,
May its captain be wise,
and may ever it return home safe.

Hymn to Njord
Rev Angela Kunschmann

Hail to Njord, the Master of Ships,
May we sail swiftly and safely.
May our nets be strong and bountiful.

Hail to Njord, Lord of Vanaheim,
May our lands be lush and fertile.
May we honor those lands as we honor Him.

Hail to Njord, the God of Temperance.
May we be as even tempered as He.
May we love all others as only He loves.

Hail to Njord, the ever-devoted Father.
May we nourish our minds, hearts, and souls as He commands.
May we love ourselves as the ocean loves the beach.

The Vegvisir
Raven Kaldera

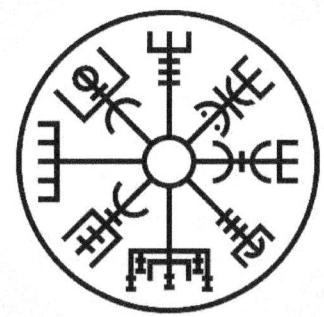

The strange mandala of symbols that we know as the Vegvisir, or "way-finder", comes to us from the Huld Manuscript. This is a collection of older charms put together in the 1880s by Geir Vigfusson, although we have no proof of when it was created, or even if it dates back past the Victorian era. As such, many Nordic practitioners choose to ignore it, because it might not be ancient.

The manuscript page states that "if this sign is carried, one will never lose one's way in storms or bad weather, even when the way is not known." Its most obvious utility is that of a navigation charm – highly useful to the seafaring Nordic peoples – and thus definitely in Njord's wheelhouse, as it were. It is worthwhile to paint on boats and ships, or carry when traveling on water.

However, according to the personal gnosis of many people, the Vegvisir is also useful as a magical compass to the Nine Worlds. In this way, it could be used to soul-journey to a specific world by mentally pointing one stave ahead of you before you go into trance. So I asked the Gods which stave was which, and I got the message that Midgard is the center point, with the other eight worlds surrounding it. In order, from the top and moving clockwise, they are:

1) Asgard
2) Svartalfheim/Nidavellir
3) Muspellheim
4) Helheim
5) Vanaheim
6) Alfheim
7) Niflheim
8) Jotunheim

Njord made it clear that I should write up this information for this book, but what He wouldn't let me write is how to use it in this capacity. His comment was: "People need to explore things. Let them be challenged. You've told them what stave is what; now let them journey themselves to learn what that means. It has many keys for many different people." So now I lay this ambivalent symbol in your laps to work with. May your quest be fruitful.

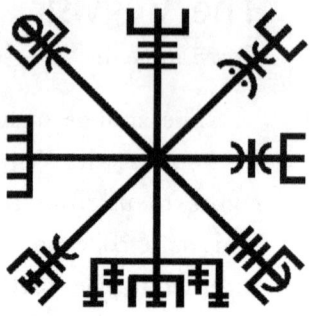

A Prayer to Njord
Susannah Ravenswing

Sea-Father, I hail you!
Let me not fear, as I go forth upon the Deep.
Lay fast Your hand on mine,
That I might set my sails sure unto the wind.
Brace my back,
That I may hold the tiller true upon my course.
Call forth Your gathered gifts into my nets,
That I may bring Your bounty back to hearth and kin.
Cradle my boat with tender care,
As You did Your own children,
That she might dance upon the waves
And bring me safely home to those I love.

Njord Ritual: Blessing a Father-To-Be
Geordie Ingerson

While the woman may bear and nurse the child, the man who has aided her in this act should also stand forth and be blessed, for he has a long and arduous, though joyful, task ahead of him. He should be blessed with salt water, and marked with the runes Uruz and Laguz, and a wreath of twigs bound with blue and white ribbons should be placed on his head.

If the man who has sired the babe will not come forth to do his job, or if he is not fit for the task, and if another (whether man or woman) has chosen to step forth and love and care for mother and babe, then let this one be blessed in his place, and simply omit the first two lines of the following prayer.

> Blessed be the fruit of thy loins.
> Blessed be the seed of thy body.
> Goodfather Njord, have you hale and healthy,
> Goodfather Njord, see you strong and sound,
> Goodfather Njord, keep you joyous on your journey,
> To love and care for your mate and child
> With the eternal power of the ocean's waves.

The wreath should be hung above the doorway of the house, where it can be seen every day when going out, as a reminder of the sacred task that has been taken on.

Njord's Frith Prayer
Michaela Macha

Njord, peace-weaver, pledge of the Vanir,
Hostage of Gods, hospitality's God,
Grant us to find for the ship of our life
Safe space in your harbour, respite from all storms.
The sea-harvest's bounty, fair riches you share;
So let's to our guests be generous and gracious,
Offer them bread and salt and protection,
Let's for each other be havens of frith.

Prayer to Njord for Cooperation
Raven Kaldera

O Ship-King who keeps the peace on crowded boats
Of our ancestors and of our own lives,
A goal lies now in front of us, for which we all now long,
But this goal will take the cooperation of many hands,
Both those who control, and those who are controlled,
Those who cage, and those who are caged.
O Lighthouse God who keeps the boats
From running aground on treacherous shoals,
Help us to see when those rocky shores approach
And guide us through the dangerous channels,
That we might not run this work aground
On constant arguments that cannot be solved.
O Fisher-King who casts your nets far and wide,
Whose flocks are silver herds, each elusive,
Cast your net of calm and willing help
Over all souls here, and bring in those folk
Who will be a benefit to gain our goals.
O Captain's God who shows leaders how to make peace
Between warring parties, show our leaders this course
And navigate them across the roughest seas.
O Njord, Ship-King of Vanaheim
Who gave yourself as a hostage to end a war,
Show us how to find cooperation
Among the many warring parties in this field of battle.

Fish Wife's Salmon Chowder
December Fields-Bryant

Njord's offerings are Salt and Protection, Prosperity of Work in the Sea. This soup is an offering to him and those that pray to him. May it nourish the body and bring warmth between those that share it.

Time: About 60 minutes including prep
Yields 4 to 6 servings

Ingredients:

- 4 ounces bacon, chopped
- 3-4 ribs celery, sliced
- 4 medium Yukon gold potatoes, cut into 1 1/2-inch cubes
- 2 cups chicken stock
- 2 1/4 cups water
- 1/2 teaspoon salt
- 2 bay leaves
- 2 sprigs of fresh thyme
- 1 Tbsp butter
- 1lb of trimmed, skinned and de-boned, salmon fillet, cut into 1-inch cubes
- 2 Tbsp flour (use rice flour if cooking gluten-free)
- A pinch of ground black pepper
- 3/4 cup (6 ounces) heavy cream
- 1/2 teaspoon lemon zest

1. Place bacon in a thick-bottomed 5 to 6-quart pot. Heat on medium to medium high heat. Cook until lightly browned and the fat mostly rendered out of the bacon, about 5 to 6 minutes. Remove all but 1 Tbsp of the bacon fat.

2. Add the celery and leeks to the bacon and cook on medium heat until softened, about 5 to 6 minutes.

3. Add diced potatoes, chicken stock, water, salt, bay leaves, and thyme to the pot. Increase heat to bring to a simmer. Then lower the heat

to maintain a gentle simmer. Simmer for 10 to 15 minutes, until the potatoes are cooked through.

4. While the potatoes are cooking, prepare the salmon. Place salmon in a bowl, sprinkle with flour and black pepper. Toss to coat. Melt butter in a non-stick skillet on medium high heat. Lightly brown the salmon on both sides.

5. When the potatoes are cooked through, use a slotted spoon to transfer the salmon to the pot with the potatoes, bacon, leeks, and stock. Cook gently for 5 minutes then remove from heat. Stir in the cream and lemon zest. Salt and pepper to taste.

Serve with a chunk of crusty homemade bread. Beer bread made from a pale, bitter ale is very appropriate.

Blue-Eyed Sailor
Seawalker

The brass compass in my pocket reminds me
Of how far we have to go. Your blue eyes twinkle
In my mind, the myriad wrinkles a map of fjords
Laid down by centuries of joy and sorrow. Hands
Grip firmly on the ship's wheel, spinning it
Like the wheel of the year, the seasons, the world
Which may seem to change little, out here on the blue
Neverending plain, but you know better. There are
Seasons here, like any other. The salt air has a tang
Unique to each. The herds of fish run at expected times,
Or did until we fished them out, wasted hundreds
Of your flocks with our mess and greed. The Sea-Gods
Whom you wave to as you sail, they have taken to
Ramming our land with their wrath, to get our attention.
You are more forgiving, Fish-Herd, but do you weep
Grey tears to see what we have done? Cod, near gone,
The bluefin but a sliver, the halibut and snapper hardly in
The nets. Do you protect the last few, in some secret
Underwater pen, waiting for us to give up on the
Emptied oceans so that you may breed again your flocks?
I hope so, Keel-Lord, though it is more than we deserve.
May we turn our compasses around and look into
Our own folly, and fish it down instead. O blue-eyed sailor God
Who protects each small family man in the tiny wooden
Boat, competing with the great machines, protect them still
Until we prove ourselves good shepherds of more
Than neverending greed.

German Fish Hotpot
Traditional

You will need:

- 2 lbs of fish fillet - bass, cod, or whiting
- ½ tsp salt
- 6 to 8 peeled, boiled, and mashed potatoes
- 1 stick of butter
- 1 onion, chopped
- Pinch of pepper
- 2 small cans anchovy fillets, mashed finely or pureed
- 3 tsp German mustard
- 1 sour pickle, thinly sliced

Poach the fillets in salted water for around eight minutes, until they are firm but still tender. Drain them, flake them, and mix with the mashed potatoes. Melt the butter and cook the onion, then add the pepper, anchovy, and mustard to make a sauce. Make a mound of the potato and fish mash, pour the sauce over it, and garnish with pickle slices.

Ocean Father
Michelle, Northern Tamarisk

Foaming father,
Ocean-wise,
Sails billow
With your sighs.

The ocean winds
Sing your songs,
For that is where
Your heart belongs.

Master of water,
When you draw near,
The fishermen
Your name do cheer.

Your golden children
Fill the stores,
You bring your bounty
To our shores.

You fill the nets,
They fill the carts,
Men's bellies are filled,
And their hearts.

Your presence blesses
All this land,
The gifts of plenty
Show your hand.

In our lives,
On our tables too.
For your many gifts
We say thank you.

Boat Blessing Charm
Geordie Ingerson

If you have a boat of any sort, make a Njord good-luck-at-sea charm for it. I've used the following items:

- A small bag of blue cloth, filled with earth from a sacred place in your home area and a single cooked fishbone, for safe return home. Tie to it:
- A small charm shaped like a ship for soundness.
- A small charm shaped like a fish for good luck.
- A white string with seven knots for good weather.
- A small wooden disc burned with Njord's bind rune—a combination of Laguz (water) and Ehwaz (horse; the boat is a water-steed). Basically, it looks like the M-shaped Ehwaz rune with its vertical "posts" also being the uprights for a forward-and-backward Laguz, so it's an Ehwaz with little tails off of each side.

Hang it in the cabin of the boat, or carry it with you when you go on the water. The first time that you take your charm onto your boat, pour out some gin overboard as an offering to him. If you have friends with boats—and especially friends who use their boats commercially, for fishing or for passengers—make one for them as a gift (along with the gin and the instructions). Njord's blessing is a good thing to carry.

The Drowned Dead of the Great Lakes
Sarenth Odinsson

The hungry waters surge
As full of the Undines as any ocean.

Ran and Her Daughters
Drag another down to icy depths.

Each Lake a Goddess—
Superior, Michigan, Huron, Ontario, Erie.

As with all the seas,
Hungry and bountiful, gifting and taking.

Be with them, O Njord,
As they join the Dead of the Great Lakes.

Bless them, O Njord,
and help their families to know peace.

O Ship-builder, O Safe Harbor,
Help them to reach their shores in comfort.

O Dead of the Great Lakes,
Each lighthouse calls you home to shore.

O Dead of the Great Lakes,
You are not forgotten, even though the cold waters claim you.

O Dead of the Great Lakes,
Your names are etched in heart and metal, paper and ink.

O Dead of the Great Lakes,
You are remembered.

For the Ship-King
Peter Ringo

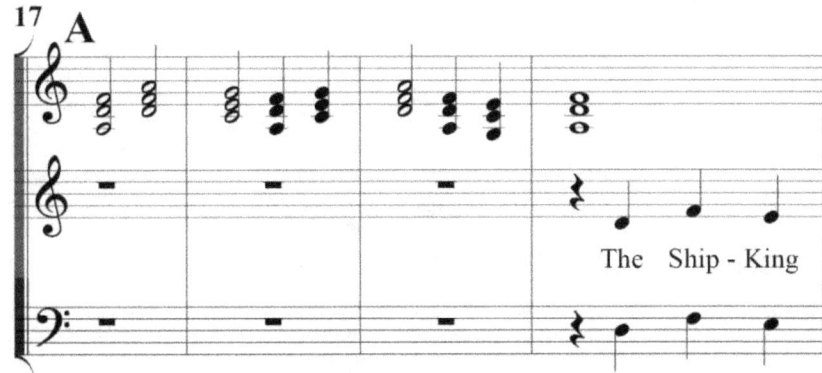
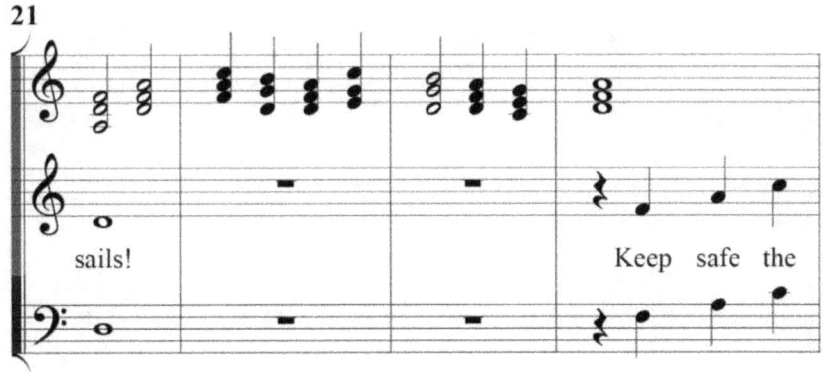

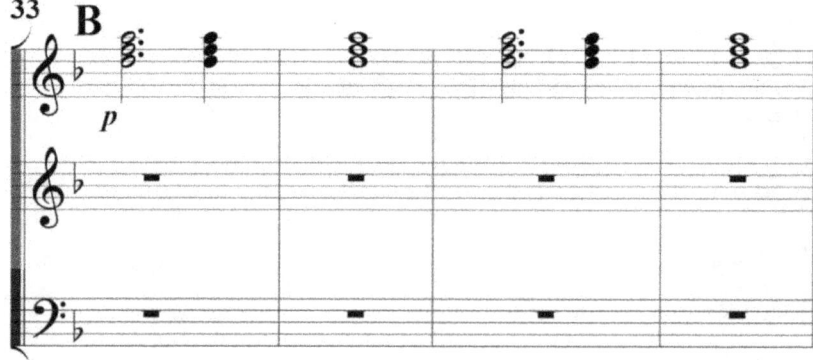

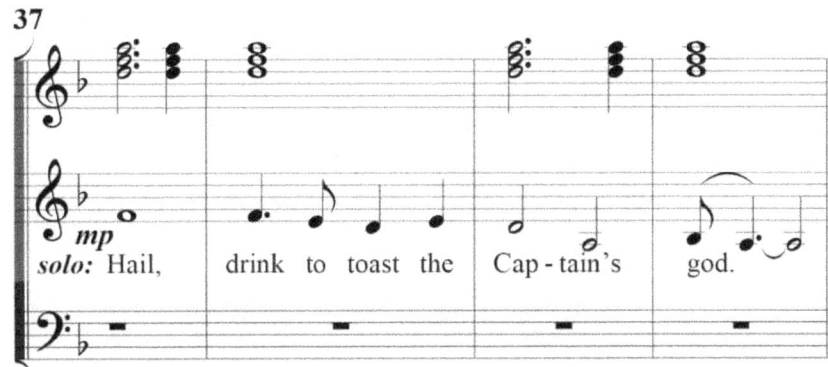

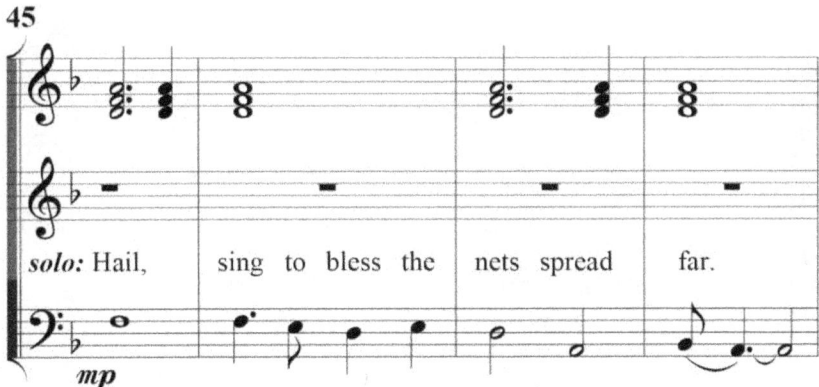

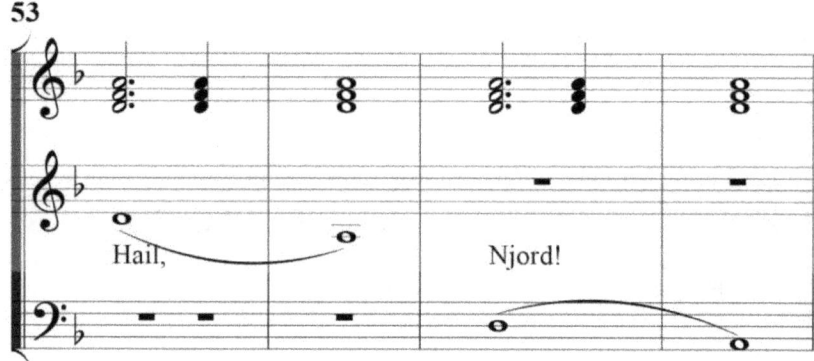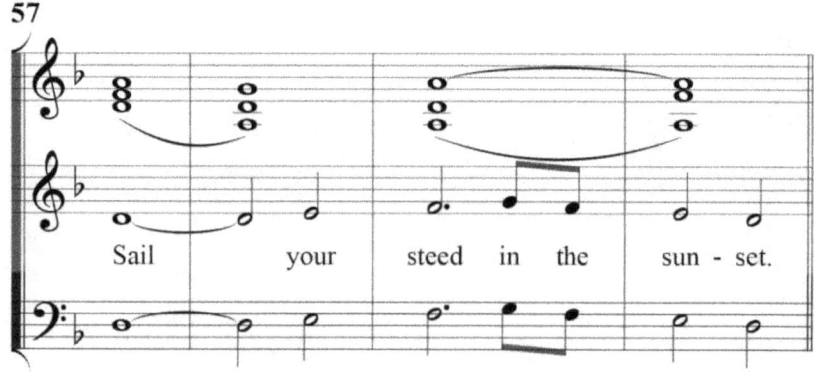

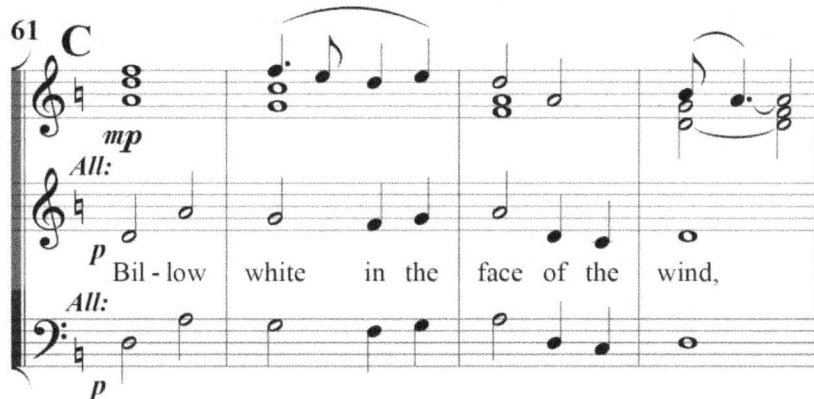

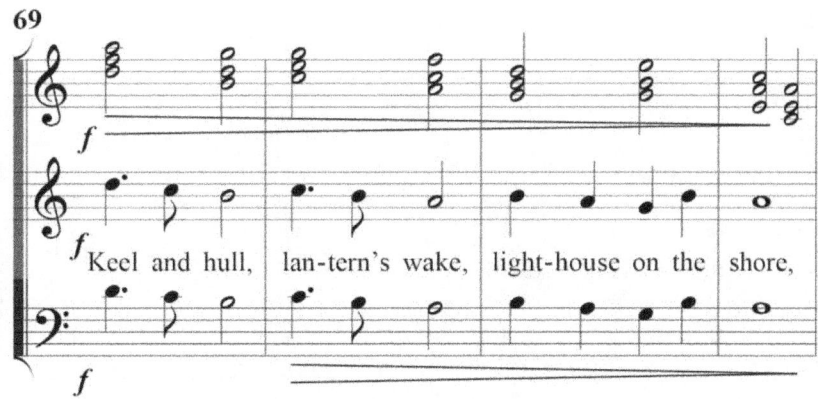

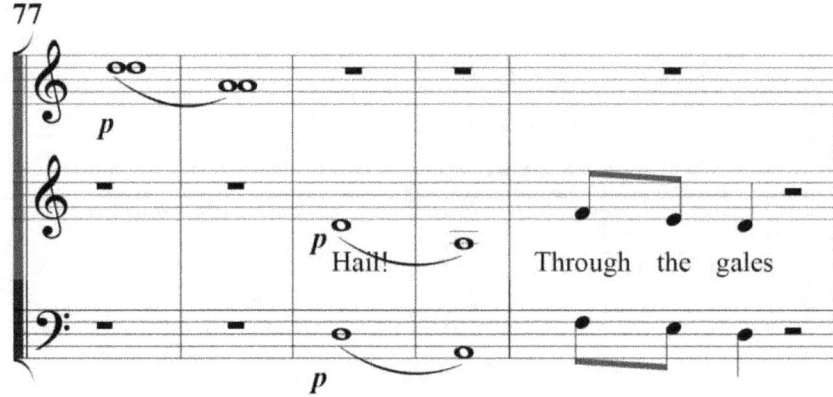
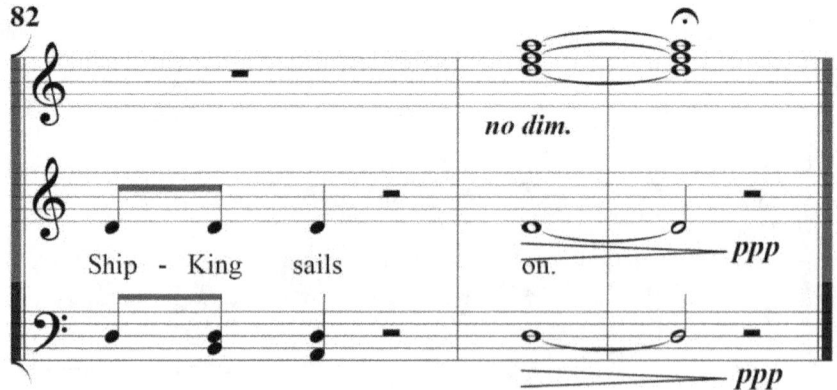

www.ingramcontent.com/pod-product-compliance
Lightning Source LLC
Chambersburg PA
CBHW031636160426
43196CB00006B/436